fresh from the clothesline

quilts and small projects
with vintage appeal

Darlene Zimmerman

KRAUSE PUBLICATIONS
Cincinnati, Ohio

table of contents

introduction

Fresh from the Clothesline brings to mind a number of images. It could suggest freshly laundered clothes or quilts blowing on an old-fashioned clothesline and smelling of sunshine and green grass. Or it could mean fresh ideas with a nod to the past. Both images are correct—fresh projects from my hands and heart to you, and a fresh way of looking at vintage-style projects for your home.

A few years ago a display of my quilts hung at a major quilt show. Many people came up to me and expressed their pleasure in seeing my quilts. "Real quilts," they said, stating that the quilts reminded them of their grandmas or their pasts. Others commented that the quilts "made them happy." Although most of the projects shown in this book are made in 1930s-reproduction fabrics, they could fit in anyone's home, regardless of their decorating style. If the pastel '30s fabrics aren't your favorite, make the projects in fabrics of your choice for a new twist (see the project variations on pages 21, 33, 51, 65, 97 and 101). All the projects are "real quilts," and the sweet pastels are bound to put a smile on your face.

From my hands and heart to yours—**happy stitching!**

Darlene

chapter

1

Small Projects

Do you need a gift in a hurry? Make up the *Trio of Towels* or the *Mommy-and-Me Aprons*. Or perhaps you need a little project for your home to brighten up a room? Try *My Sweet Table Runner* or the *Dresden-Plate Table Topper*. Sometimes a small project is just what you need for a break when working on a large quilt or when your days are too busy to work on a big project. These small projects are "just right" to make for a quick gift or a special treat for yourself.

sailboat
PILLOW

This whimsical pillow makes use of rickrack for waves and a bit of ribbon for a flag. Quick to piece—just one boat—it is also easy to finish, as the front and back are sewn together and bound like a quilt, creating a faux corded-edge finish. For a completely different look, make this pillow in different fabrics for an older sailor in your life.

cutting directions

from	cut	yield
yellow print	one 12½"×42" strip	two 12½"×17" rectangles
		one 4"×6½" rectangle
		one 4"×4½" rectangle
background	two 4"×42" strips	one 4"×8" rectangle
		one 4"×6½" rectangle
		one 4"×4½" rectangle
		one 3½"×8" rectangle
		one 2½"×2½" square
		two 2½"×4" rectangles
		one 1½"×6" rectangle
		one 1"×6" rectangle
		one 1"×6½" rectangle
blue print	one 3"×21" strip	one 3"×12½" rectangle
red print	one 2½"×42" strip	one 2½"×10½" rectangle
	two 3¼"×42" strips	binding

materials

fabric requirements

yellow print: ⅜ yd.
red print: ⅓ yd.
blue print: fat eighth
background: ¼ yd.
backing: 14" square
batting: 14" square

suggested tool

*Tri-Recs (EZ Quilting #8823753)

additional requirements

14" jumbo rickrack, blue
2" of ½" wide ribbon (optional)
12" pillow form

finished dimensions

12" square

*If not using the Tri-Recs tool, use template on page 13.

assembling
the pillow top

1. Layer the yellow print and background 4"×6½" rectangles both wrong sides up. Cut one Recs pair (please see Recs template). Sew the triangles right sides together. Press toward the yellow triangle. *(figure 1)*

2. Layer the yellow print and background 4"×4½" rectangles both right sides up. Cut one Recs pair. Sew the triangles right sides together. Press toward the yellow triangle. *(figure 2)*

3. Place the 2½"×4" background rectangles right sides together on both ends of the red rectangle as shown. Sew and trim the seam allowance to ¼", and press toward the red rectangle. Trim the unit evenly to 2½"×12½". *(figure 3)*

4. Sew the blue rectangle to the bottom of the boat *(step 3)*. Press the seam open. Sew the rickrack over the seam with a narrow zigzag stitch in matching thread. *(figure 4)*

5. Using the diagram, sew the shapes for the top half of the block together. Sew the short end of the ribbon in the seam as shown in the illustration. *(figure 5)* Press. Sew the top and bottom boat pieces together. Press.

figure 1

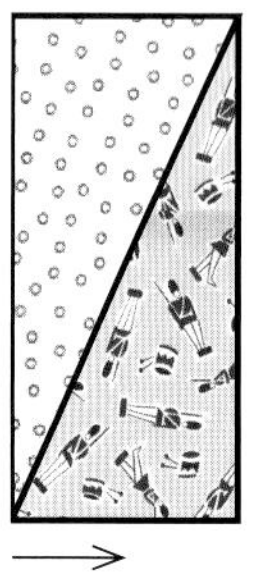

figure 2

figure 3

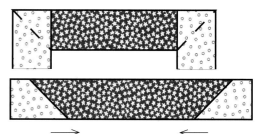

figure 4

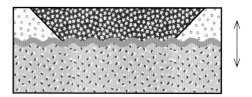

figure 5

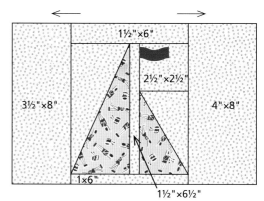

finishing
the pillow

1. Fold and press the 2 yellow print 12½"×17" rectangles in half to make two 8½"×12½" rectangles. Overlap the folded edges to make a square that measures 12½". Baste around the edges to keep the pillow back together. *(figure 6)*

2. Layer the pillow front right-side up with the batting and the backing. Baste and then quilt as desired.

3. With right sides out, baste the pillow top and back together ¼" around the edge. Do not trim the excess batting and backing until after the binding has been sewn on.

4. Sew the two 3¼" wide red print binding strips together with a diagonal seam pressed open. Press in half, wrong sides together, for a double binding. Sew to the pillow with a ⅜" seam, mitering the corners. (See page 119 for mitering corners. See page 120-121 for joining the binding ends.)

5. Trim the excess batting and backing at least ¼" beyond the edge of the binding to make the binding look fuller. Turn the binding to the back side and stitch down by hand with matching thread. Insert the pillow form, and your pillow is now finished!

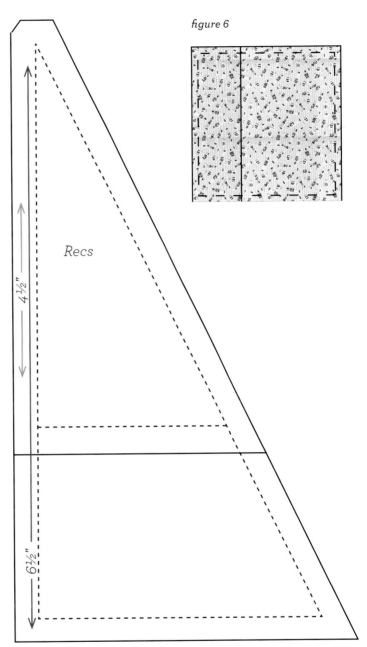

figure 6

Recs

4½"

6½"

Recs template

REVERSIBLE PARTY
place mats

These place mats are fun to make! The front sides of the place mats are sewn in a kaleidoscope design, easily made with strip sets and cut with a 45° Triangle. By using a party-hat fabric on the back side of the place mats, you need only flip them over for a special event. One of the four place mats has a different color back to denote the "birthday person" or the person being honored. Whip up a set of these place mats to use every day and for special events!

cutting directions for two place mats

from	cut	yield
prints 1–4	five 2"×21" strips	strip sets
yellow print	one 4"×21" strip	eight Easy Angle* triangles
blue print	four 2¼"×42" strips	binding

*If not using Easy Angle tool, cut four 4⅜" squares; cut once on the diagonal.

cutting directions for four place mats

from	cut	yield
prints 1–4	five 2"×42" strips	ten 2"×21" strips for strip sets
yellow print	one 4"×42" strip	16 Easy Angle* triangles*
blue print	seven 2¼"×42" strips	binding

*If not using Easy Angle tool, cut eight 4⅜" squares; cut once on the diagonal.

materials

fabric requirements

2 PLACE MATS
prints 1–4: fat quarters
binding: ⅓ yd.
backing: ⅜ yd.
batting: 15"×42"

4 PLACE MATS
prints 1–3: ⅓ yd. each
yellow print 4: ½ yd.
binding: ½ yd.
backing 1: ⅞ yd.
backing 2: fat quarter
batting: 30"×42"

suggested tools

Easy Angle (EZ Quilting #8829412)

*45° Triangle (EZ Quilting #8829421)

finished dimensions

19"×12½"

*If not using the 45° Triangle tool, use template on page 17.

assembling the place mats
(numbers for 4 place mats in parentheses)

1. Sew the 2"×21" strips together into strip sets, keeping the fabrics in the same order in each strip set. Press the seams all one direction. Make 5 (10) strip sets. *(figure 1)*

2. Using the 45° Triangle, cut 16 (32) 6½" triangles from the strip sets as shown. *(figure 2)*

3. Cut the remaining strip sets into 8 (16) 4" wide units. Set aside for borders. *(figure 3)*

4. Alternating the triangles, sew together in identical pairs. Press the seams all one direction. *(figure 4)*

5. Sew the pairs from Step 4 together, making half circles. *(figure 5)* Sew the halves together, pinning and matching the center and seams. Pop a few stitches in the center so the seam allowances spin around the center. Press. Make 2 (4) blocks.

6. Turn each of the blocks so the outer green strips are in the corners. Center and sew triangles to all four corners of each block. Press toward the center of the block. Make 2 (4) blocks. At this point the blocks should measure 12½". *(figure 6)*

7. Sew the border strip units together in pairs, with the green rectangles in the center. Sew the units to opposite sides of the blocks completed in Step 6. Make 2 (4) place mats. Press.

figure 1

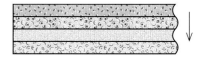

figure 2

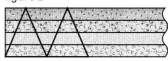

figure 3

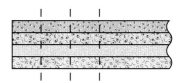

figure 4

figure 5

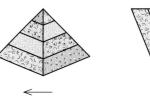
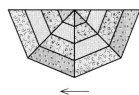

figure 6

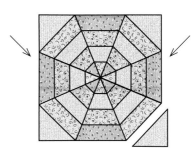

finishing the
place mats

1. Layer, baste and quilt. If making the set of four place mats, use Backing to designate the person being honored. You can machine stitch in the ditch on each "spoke" of the circle and between the rectangles in the borders.

2. Before binding, baste a scant ¼" from the edge of the place mats to keep the layers together. Sew the binding ends together with diagonal seams pressed open. Fold in half wrong sides together and press to make a double binding. Sew to the place mats with a ¼" seam, mitering the corners (see pages 119-121 for mitering and joining binding ends). Trim the excess batting and backing, and turn the binding to the back side; stitch down by hand with matching thread.

45° Triangle

6½"

Place Mats & Tablecloths

We don't know the origin of place mats, but as a busy woman, don't you appreciate how quickly you can set a table with place mats? They add color and flair to your table. A tablecloth can be used instead, but one spill or spot, and the whole tablecloth needs to be washed. These *Reversible Party Place Mats* can be quickly washed and probably will not need ironing!

In the 1930s era, women would have used colorful tablecloths or set a pretty table with their prized colorful glassware that we know today as "Depression glass." Depression glass refers to the clear or colored glass manufactured from the late 1920s through the early 1940s. It was pretty, it was cheerful in the rainbow of pastel colors and a variety of patterns, and it added a happy note to some very dismal days of the Great Depression and World War II. It was made from mass-produced molded glass of rather poor quality with air bubbles and heavy molding marks. It was also inexpensive. At your local dime store you could purchase a piece for about five cents—the same cost as a loaf of bread. The glassware was also offered as premiums for a larger purchase or tucked into oatmeal or detergent boxes. Gas stations even offered a punch bowl and cups with an oil change! Even movie theaters got on the bandwagon, giving away a piece of glassware with a Saturday matinee ticket. Although these pieces were inexpensive, they are now very collectible and treasured—and still set a pretty table.

MY SWEET
table runner

The Double Wedding Ring pattern is probably the most recognized quilt pattern. Even nonquilters can recognize and name the pattern. It's also the most requested quilt pattern by brides. Are you hesitant to make one? Don't be. This three-ring table runner is a good size for you to try out the pattern and template set to see if you wish to make a large quilt. You may be pleasantly surprised at how easily it goes together!

cutting directions

A "Double Wedding Ring" tool is required for this project.

from	cut	yield
background	three 10¼" squares	three large squares cut with the DWR tool
yellow solid	one 7¼"×42" strip	ten melons cut with the DWR tool
from each of two prints	two 2⁹⁄₁₆"×21" strips	ten 2⁹⁄₁₆" squares cut with the DWR tool
from each of the six prints	three 2¾"×21" strips	four "B" wedges
		four "B" reversed wedges
		20 "A" wedges
yellow solid	1¼" bias strips	binding

Note: You can choose the placement of each print or mix them randomly.

materials

fabric requirements

background fabric: ⅜ yd.

yellow solid fabric for melons and binding: ⅝ yd.

six assorted prints: fat eighths

two prints for corner squares: fat eighths

backing: 1¼ yds.

batting: 45"×21"

required tool

Double Wedding Ring (EZ Quilting #8829419)

finished dimensions

18½"×43½"

piecing directions

1. Sew 6 "A" wedges together. Add a "B" wedge and a reversed "B" wedge to both ends. Repeat to make a total of 20 arcs. (Some "Bs" will be left over.) *(figure 1)*

2. Using one set of arcs from Step 1, sew the arc to a melon, matching centers and ends and pinning before sewing. Press toward the melon. Repeat for a set of ten arcs. *(Tip: Sew with the melon on top.) (figure 2)*

3. Using the second set of arcs, sew a different color 2⅜" square to each end. Press the seams all one direction. *(figure 3)* Sew to the Step 2 units, pressing toward the melons. Make a total of ten melon/arc units. *(figure 4)*

4. Pinning and matching centers and ends, sew the melon/arc units from Step 3 to the large squares. *(figure 5)* Press the seams toward the square. Sew three melon/arc units to adjacent sides of two squares.

5. Pinning and sewing as in Step 4, sew melon/ arc units to all four sides of the remaining large square. Sew this unit between the Step 4 units. Press the seams toward the squares.

finishing the table runner

1. Trim the backing and batting to 45"×21". Layer and baste. Quilt as desired. The runner shown was machine meandered in the background areas and stitched in the ditch between the wedges and the squares and also around the melons and large squares.

2. Baste a scant ¼" by hand or with a walking foot on the machine around the edge of the table runner to hold the layers together and prevent distortion.

3. Join the bias-binding strips (see page 118 for instructions on cutting bias binding) with diagonal seams pressed open. Sew the single binding to the runner with a ¼" seam, pivoting at the V between the rings with the needle down and lifting the presser foot. *Do not* stitch any pleats into the binding (see page 122). Join ends with "Perfect Fit" Binding (pages 120–121).

4. Trim the excess batting and backing to an even ¼" seam allowance. Turn the binding under ¼" and fold over the edge, covering the stitching line on the back side. The binding should form a pleat in the V. Stitch down by hand with matching thread.

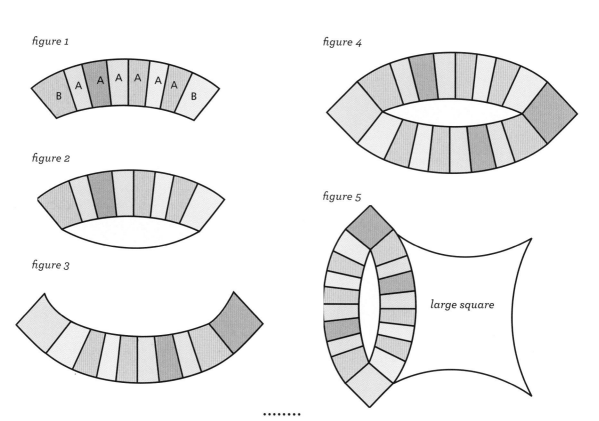

figure 1

figure 2

figure 3

figure 4

figure 5

large square

variation:
DOUBLE WEDDING RING

The classic Double Wedding Ring pattern uses the 1930s prints with either a white or solid-colored background. But consider all the possibilities! In this variation I used a fat quarter bundle of purple and gray solids and graduated the colors from light to dark. I hand-quilted with a dark gray thread to add more depth and interest to the solid fabrics.

cutting directions

A "Double Wedding Ring" tool is required for this project.

cut three 10¼" squares from gray solid;
cut three centers with the DWR template

cut one 7¼" × 42" strip from
gray solid; cut ten melons

cut 20 wedges from each of the six lightest solids

cut 20 "B" wedges and 20 reversed
"B" wedges from the next darkest solid

cut ten squares each from two the next darkest
solids using the DWR tool

Binding: Cut the remainder of the darkest fat quarter into 1¼" wide bias-binding strips. Join with diagonal seams pressed open. Sew to the quilt with a ¼" seam allowance.

materials

fabric requirements

background & backing: ⅝ yd. gray solid

purple solids: 9 fat quarters in graduated colors

binding: remainder of darkest solid used

backing: 1¼ yds.

batting: 23" × 46"

TABLETOP
tree skirt

Not all Christmas trees are big. The small tabletop trees also need to have a tree skirt. Make up the tree skirt in any holiday prints and embellish as you choose, and it will be finished in no time!

cutting directions

A "Fat Cats" tool is required for this project.

cut one 12"×42" strip from both holiday fabrics

• •

cut six Fat Cat wedges from both holiday fabrics

• •

If the holiday fabric is directional, you will be able to use only every other wedge; cut twelve wedges instead of six. Use the wedges that have the motifs right-side up.

materials

fabric requirements

dark holiday print: ⅜ yd.
light holiday print: ⅜ yd.
note: if holiday prints are directional, buy ¾ yd. of each
accent print: fat quarter
batting: 30" square
backing: ⅞ yd.

suggested tool

*Easy Scallop (EZ Quilting #8823754)

required tool

Fat Cats (EZ Quilting #8823747)

additional requirements

red baby rickrack (optional)

finished dimensions

26" diameter

If you don't have the Easy Scallop tool, you can use a lid or a plate from your kitchen to mark and trim a curved edge.

assembling the table topper/ tree skirt

1. Sew the wedges together, alternating colors. Press the seams open if adding rickrack over the seams. Add rickrack if desired.

2. Layer the backing wrong-side up, the batting and the tree skirt right-side up. Baste. Quilt as desired. (The tree skirt shown is stitched in lines radiating out from the center.)

3. Using the largest Easy Scallop tool set at 7", round out the pointed corners at each seam intersection. Use the tool to mark only; then trim with scissors or use the lines as a placement guide when sewing on the binding.

4. Using the accent fabric fat quarter, cut 2¼" wide bias binding. Join the ends with diagonal seams pressed open. Press the binding in half, wrong sides together. Sew the binding to the edge of the tree skirt. Join with the "Perfect Fit" binding technique on (see pages 120-121).

5. Trim the excess batting and backing, turn the binding to the back side and stitch down by hand with matching thread.

6. Trim the remainder of the binding to 1¼" wide. Press out the crease and press the short end under ¼". Sew the single binding to the inner circle, overlapping the beginning edge. Trim and stitch down on the backside.

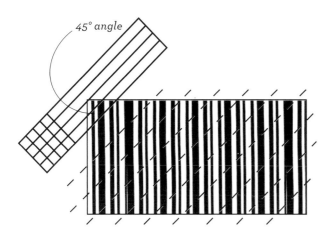

45° angle

Cutting bias binding

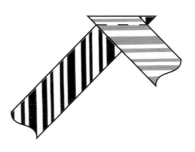

Joining diagonal ends

The Real Story of Rudolph the Red-Nosed Reindeer

Rudolph was "born" in 1939 when Robert May, employed by Montgomery Ward in Chicago (you all remember the catalog and department stores), was asked to come up with a Christmas story for a promotional giveaway over the holidays. May came up with the idea of a reindeer teased by his friends because of his glowing red nose. In choosing a name for this reindeer, he considered Rollo and Reginald but finally decided upon Rudolph. He wrote Rudolph's story in verse, testing it out on his four-year-old daughter, Barbara. His daughter loved the story, but May's boss was worried that Rudolph's red nose would be associated with drunkards—not a suitable topic for children.

To convince his boss to use his story, May asked Denver Gillen from Montgomery Ward's art division to the Chicago Zoo to draw reindeer. The reindeer Gillen drew were so cute that May's boss was won over, and the story was approved. The story of Rudolph the Red-Nosed Reindeer was such a hit that Montgomery Ward distributed 2.4 million copies of the story that year.

A few years later, after World War II ended, there was a great demand for licensing the Rudolph character. However, Montgomery Ward held the copyright, so May received no royalties on the character he had created. Unfortunately May's wife died from a serious illness, leaving May in debt. He pleaded with Montgomery Ward's president to turn the copyright over to him in 1947—and Montgomery Ward did so. Then May's future was secured. The story was printed commercially after that.

May's brother-in-law, Johnny Marks, a songwriter, developed the lyrics and melody for the song we know so well today. Finally they found Gene Autry to record the song (many others turned them down), and the song became the second-best-selling song of all time (behind "White Christmas"). In 1964 the television special we've all seen was produced and is still being shown every Christmas.

May was able to leave his job at Montgomery Ward in 1951 to spend the next seven years managing "Rudolph." Then he returned to work at Montgomery Ward and worked there until his retirement in 1971.

Interestingly enough, the story May wrote was different from the story we are familiar with. May's Rudolph was not one of Santa's reindeer, nor did he live at the North Pole. He may have been teased for his red nose, but he came from a loving family who gave him a good self-image. In May's story, Rudolph was picked by Santa quite by accident when Santa noticed Rudolph's red glowing nose in the thickening fog on Christmas Eve. At their safe return after delivering the presents, Santa gave all the credit to Rudolph, saying, "By *you* last night's journey was actually bossed. Without you, I'm certain we'd all have been lost!"

If you'd like to read more about the icons of Christmas, read *The Trouble With Christmas* by Tom Flynn (Prometheus Books, copyright 1993). Now, can you remember the other reindeer's names on Santa's team?

TRIO OF
towels

Make your very own trio of tea towels. With such adorable towels, who wouldn't enjoy helping clean up? Add a bit of rickrack, embellishments or whatever trims you choose to make them unique.

cutting directions

trim off selvages on the print fat quarters

trim each of the print fat quarters to
measure 17"×20"

materials

fabric requirements

three prints: 1 fat
quarter each

three prints for prairie
points: ⅛ yd. or 4"×42"

three accent fabrics:
2½"×42" strips each

optional
requirement

variety of rickrack

finished dimensions

12½"×19"

Cheap Trick!

Try my cheap trick for putting together scrap quilts. After cutting all the pieces from a variety of fabrics, put the pieces you need for one block on a cheap paper plate. Do this for each of the blocks, dividing out the colors evenly, and then stack the plates. Now, when you have a few minutes to sew, everything is handy to quickly sew together a block. You can also write notes to yourself right on the plates. You'll be surprised at how quickly you finish your quilt with this method.

assembling the tea towels

1. Hem two long sides and one short end of each of the 17"×20" prints. To do this, fold the edge under a scant ¼" and press. Turn under again ¼" and press. Topstitch the hem. Leave one short end unfinished.

2. From each of the prints for the prairie points, cut six 4" squares.

3. Fold each of the 4" squares in half once on the diagonal and press. Fold again on the diagonal and press again to make prairie points. *(figure 1)*

4. Trim each of the accent plaid strips into two 2½"×16½" strips (or exactly ½" more than the width of the towel).

5. For each of the towels, align the prairie points (tucked inside one another) right sides together on one long edge of one accent strip. The prairie points should come right to the corner and not extend beyond it. Baste in place with a scant ¼" seam. *(figure 2)*

6. Place the second matching accent strip right sides together with the first accent strip, sandwiching the prairie points between. Sew an exact ¼" seam along the edge with the prairie points. Press the seam away from the prairie points on both sides. Press one long edge under ¼". *(figure 3)*

7. Sew the unpressed long edge right sides together with the towel. Press the seam toward the accent strip. If you choose to add rickrack, sew it ¾" or more below the seam.

8. Fold the accent strip right sides together and sew the short ends only up to the seam allowance at the top. Turn right-side out.

9. The folded edge of the accent strip should now cover the seam on the back side of the towel. Pin in place and then topstitch along the edge of the accent strip on the right side of the towel. A quick pressing and your lovely tea towels are ready to display and use!

Optional: If desired, rickrack can be added over the seam between the towel and the accent strip. The ends are just tucked around the back and stitched in place.

figure 1

figure 2

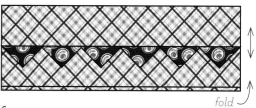

figure 3

fold

Tea Towels

I grew up on a farm—with five sisters (and no brothers!)—in Minnesota. With such a large family, there was always cooking, baking and canning going on in the kitchen. We not only ate three big meals a day but also had midmorning and midafternoon "lunches," which usually consisted of a sandwich and cookies or cake. Believe it or not, none of us had weight problems until we left home. Back then, the kitchen was truly the heart of the home and was where the family spent the most time together.

With all this cooking and baking going on, there were always quite a few dishes to wash and dry—by hand, of course, as we didn't have a dishwasher.

While people today might think this was an unpleasant chore, it often was fun. We'd catch up on each other's news, sing songs with the radio and discuss daily events. The tea towels we used then were made from white feedsacks and featured embroidered motifs; they were ideal for drying dishes. The *Trio of Towels* we're making here are more decorative but still functional.

Below you will find my favorite chocolate chip cookie recipe you can make for a snack. While you are baking them, invite your family or a friend into your kitchen to help you with the dishes (hand them a tea towel!) while you catch up on all their news.

recipe

oatmeal chocolate chip cookies

¾ cup butter

¾ cup white sugar

¾ cup brown sugar

2 eggs

1 tsp. salt

1 tsp. baking soda

1 tsp. vanilla

2 tsp. water

1½ cups flour

3 cups oatmeal

6 oz. chocolate chips (or raisins)

- Cream butter, sugar and eggs.
- Add salt, soda, vanilla and water.
- Mix, then add flour.
- Stir in oatmeal and chips.
- Drop from teaspoon onto greased cookie sheet.
- Bake at 350° F for about 12 minutes.

MOMMY-AND-ME
aprons

Aprons, aprons, aprons. These aprons are very easy to make. You'll gather and hem three rectangles and sew them together quickly. How much fun to make a set for mother and child or grammy and child!

Women had been wearing aprons for generations, but they went out of style as women entered the workforce. However, a new generation of young women has rediscovered how practical (and fun!) an apron can be.

cutting directions

child apron (child size 1–3)

tier 1	cut one 3½" × 16" rectangle
tier 2	cut one 3½" × 23" rectangle
tier 3	cut one 4" × 33" rectangle
bib	cut two 6" squares for the bib
ties	cut two 2" × 12" strips for the neck ties
	cut one 3" × 42" strip for the waist ties

mommy apron

tier 1	cut one 7¼" × 24" rectangle
tier 2 and ties	cut one 7¼" × 34" rectangle
	cut two 4" × 42" strips for the apron ties
tier 3	cut one 7¼" × 42" rectangle and one 7¼" × 12" rectangle

materials

fabric requirements

CHILD APRON
tier 1: ⅛ yd.
tier 2: ⅛ yd.
tier 3: ⅛ yd.
bib and ties: ⅓ yd.

MOMMY APRON
tier 1: ¼ yd.
tier 2 and ties: ½ yd.
tier 3: ½ yd.

additional requirements

CHILD APRON
3 small buttons
1 pkg. baby rickrack

MOMMY APRON
2 pkgs. medium rickrack

assembling the child's apron

1. Gather (using the longest stitch) the top edge of each of the tiers. Hem (fold under ¼" twice and stitch) the bottom edge of the tier 3 rectangle. Gather the top edge, match centers and sew with a ⅜" seam to the bottom edge of the tier 2 rectangle. Press the seam toward the tier 2 rectangle.

2. In the same manner, gather the top edge of the tier 2 rectangle, match centers and sew with a ⅜" seam to the bottom of the tier 1 rectangle. Press toward the tier 1 rectangle.

3. Hem the sides of the apron (as in Step 1). Add rickrack or other trims over the seam lines and to the bottom hem.

4. Gather the top edge of the apron to approximately 9". Match the middle of the apron skirt to the middle of the waist tie. Sew with a ⅜" seam.

5. Fold the raw edges of the waist tie under ⅜" and press. Fold in half the long way and press again. Topstitch ⅛" from the edge of the waist tie.

6. Place the two bib squares right sides together, then sew along three sides with a ¼" seam. Turn and then press the unstitched edges under ⅜".

7. Fold the long edges and one short edge of the two 2"×12" neck ties under ¼". Fold in half, folded edges together. Stitch ⅛" on all the folded edges.

8. Insert the ties into the top edge of the apron bib. Pin in place and then topstitch ⅛" around all the edges of the apron bib. Add two rows of rickrack to the top edge of the apron bib. Attach the apron bib to the waistband of the apron with three small buttons.

assembling the mommy's apron

1. Join the short ends of the 7¼"×42" and 7¼"×12" rectangles to make the third tier of the apron. Hem the bottom edge by folding under ¼" twice and stitching. Gather (using the longest stitch) ¼" from the top edge on each of the tiers.

2. Pull the gathers on tier 3 to match the bottom length of tier 2. Sew a ⅜" seam. Press the seam toward tier 2 (or open, if adding rickrack or other trims).

3. Gather the top edge of tier 2 to match the bottom length of tier 1. Sew together with a ⅜" seam. Press the seam toward tier 1 (or open, if adding rickrack or other trims).

4. Hem the side edges. Add rickrack to tiers 1 and 2 at this point, wrapping the ends of the rickrack around the back. *(Tip: Use a small zigzag or straight stitch and matching thread to stitch on the rickrack.)*

5. Gather the top edge of tier 1 to 17". Join the short ends of the two 4"×42" apron ties and press open. Matching the seam on the ties to the center of the apron, sew the ties to the apron with a ⅜" seam.

6. Fold the raw edges of the apron ties under ⅜" and press. Fold the apron ties in half the long way and press. Topstitch ⅛" from the folded edges of the ties. Your apron is now finished!

Aprons

Aprons were designed to cover one's garments to protect them from spots and stains while cooking and doing household chores. Have you ever ruined a good blouse or outfit by splashing spaghetti sauce on it? Or discovered white spots on your clothing from the bleach in some cleaning product? An apron could have saved the day!

Aprons were generally designed to be cover-ups because they could be washed and ironed more quickly than a dress and could therefore be changed more often. The utilitarian apron was practical, but women also sewed "fancy" aprons to wear when hosting guests or for serving at charity or church functions. A woman's "Sunday best" apron would serve a dual purpose—showing off her sewing skills and also protecting her best dress.

Most women sewed their own aprons—rickrack was a favorite trim and shows up on most of the vintage aprons you find today. Often the edges were finished with bias tape, or seams were finished or covered with purchased bias tape. Sometimes embroidery was added, or even appliqué! Some of the "fancy" apron patterns were quite involved and challenging to make.

variation:

MOMMY-AND-ME APRONS

Using black, white and red polka dots takes these aprons to a different level. Polka dots are always fun and available in a range of colors. Trim the aprons with rickrack or embellishments of your choice. To make the pattern even easier, I substituted ribbon for the apron ties.

Make the aprons the same as in the main pattern, but substitute ribbon for the waist ties on both aprons and the neck ties on the child's apron.

materials

fabric requirements

CHILD APRON

small black polka dot: ⅛ yd.

white polka dot: ⅛ yd.

large black polka dot: ⅓ yd.

⅞" wide red polka dot ribbon: ⅔ yd.

⅜" red polka dot ribbon: ⅔ yd.

3 small red ladybug buttons

medium (½") red rickrack:
1 pkg. or 1¼ yds.

MOMMY APRON

small black polka dot: ¼ yd.

white polka dot: ¼ yd.

large black polka dot: ½ yd.

1½" wide red polka dot ribbon: 2 yds.

medium (½") red rickrack:
2 pkgs. or 3¼ yds.

dresden plate
TABLE TOPPER

So easy to make—just cut wedges using the Fat Cats tool, stitch across the tops, turn and voilà! Almost done. Some quick cutting, a bit of sewing and fusing, and this project is ready for your table. It's so fun and easy to make in many fabric combinations. You'll want to make some table toppers for yourself (and a few for gifts) for every season of the year!

cutting directions

A "Fat Cats" tool is required for this project.

from each of the prints, cut one 12" strip

from each strip, cut four wedge shapes using the full length of the Fat Cats tool

Dresden Plate

The Dresden Plate pattern is actually quite old. There is a documented quilt made in the United States in 1785 that has a Dresden Plate in the center. However, it wasn't until the 1930s era that the pattern became widely popular. The name "Dresden Plate" is probably derived from the plate's resemblance to the china plates from factories in Dresden, Germany, which were highly prized in the late 1800s and early 1900s.

The oldest reference to the name *Dresden Plate* comes from Ruby McKim's *101 Patchwork Patterns* book in the late 1920s. The pattern is also called "Friendship Ring."

Dresden Plate quilts were made by the thousands in the 1930s era. It was the perfect pattern for the small-scale pastel fabrics available during that time. Most women sewed their family's clothing from 100 percent cotton fabric and therefore had many sewing scraps left over. These scraps were put to good use in patterns like the Dresden Plate.

A Dresden Plate can be any size and have any number of wedges. It can have a plain circular edge, a scalloped edge or a pointed edge. A center can be appliquéd over the middle, or the middle can be left open. Often one can find a set of vintage Dresden Plates not appliquéd to a background. Upon closer inspection you may find they do not lie flat because the person who made them did not have an accurate template. We have an advantage over those women—we have Easy Dresden and Fat Cats tools that are multisized and can be used with a rotary cutter.

materials

fabric requirements

3 coordinating prints:
⅜ yd. each
backing: ⅓ yd.

suggested tool

Bamboo Pointer/
Creaser (EZ Quilting
#882108)

required tool

Fat Cats (EZ Quilting
#8823747)

additional requirements

freezer paper: 4" square
fusible web: 1⅓ yds.

finished dimensions

26" across

piecing directions

1. Fold the widest edge of the wedge right sides together and sew a ¼" seam across the top using a short stitch (to eliminate backstitching). Trim off the corner and turn the point (the bamboo pointer/creaser works perfectly for this task). Repeat for each of the wedges. *(figure 1)*

2. Press the wedge shapes, centering the point in the middle of the wedge. *(figure 2)*

3. Arrange the wedge shapes in a circle (12 wedges make up a circle) and then sew together with a ¼" seam. Start at the widest edges about ½" from the folded edge, backstitch to the edge and then stitch forward (this hides the thread ends). Press the seams all one direction around the circle. *(figure 3)*

4. To finish the center, cut a template circle from freezer paper *(figure 5)* and iron to the wrong side of the fabric chosen for the center. Cut out, adding ¼" seam allowance. Wet the seam allowance with spray starch and a Q-tip and iron the edges over the freezer-paper circle. Remove the freezer paper. Fold the circle into quarters, creasing lightly. Use the fold lines to center the circle on the Dresden Plate. Appliqué in place by hand or machine over the center of the Dresden Plate. Or, use the fusible web for the appliqué.

Note: If using fusible web, fuse the center circle in place after the backing has been added.

finishing the table topper

1. To add a backing, place the finished Dresden Plate on top of the fusible web, making sure the straight edge of the fusible web is about ½" below the center seam (half of the Dresden Plate).

2. With a pencil, make a dot at each *V* of the wedges. Remove the Dresden Plate, and with a ruler, connect the dots, forming an uneven half circle. *(figure 4)*

3. Cut out the fusible web on the marked line and, using this as a template, make a second identical fusible shape. Cut out the second half. Fuse both halves of the fusible web to the wrong side of the backing fabric.

4. Peel off the paper backing from one half, position the backing in place over half of the Dresden Plate and fuse, following the manufacturer's directions for fusing. (*Tip: Before fusing the backing to the Dresden Plate, check the fit on the front side of the Dresden Plate. Trim as necessary.*)

5. Repeat for the other half of the backing, overlapping at the center. If using a fused circle for the center, add this now.

6. Add any decorative or invisible stitching around the center at this time if desired. Your table topper is now complete!

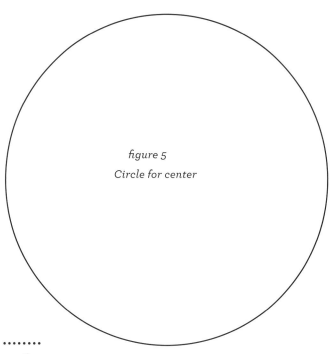

figure 5
Circle for center

figure 1   figure 2   figure 3

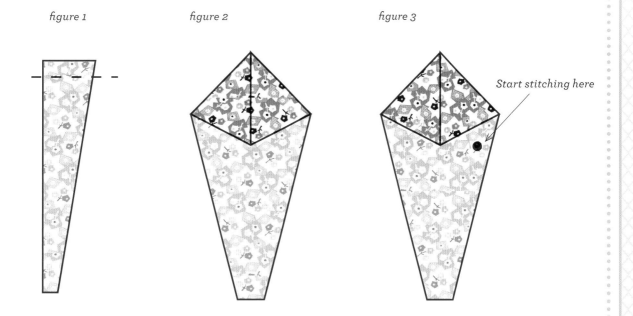

Start stitching here

figure 4

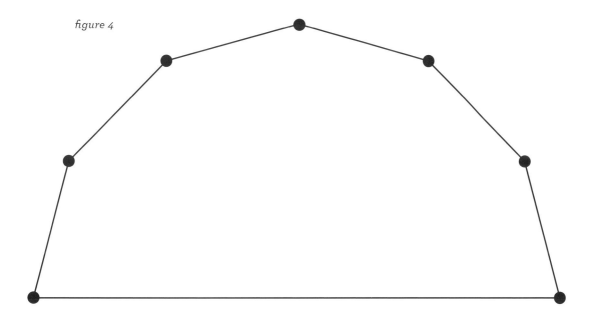

chapter

2

Small Quilts

When trying a new tool or technique, it's often best to start with a smaller project to see how well you like it. Or, if you don't need a big quilt right now, a small- to medium-sized quilt is perfect for your next project. Try out some new techniques—make some crazy quilt blocks (as in the *Simply Crazy Quilt*), try setting some blocks "wonky" (as in the *Wonky-Stars Wall Hanging*) or play with hexagons and 60-degree triangles (as in *Grammy's Garden*). Break out of your box and try a new technique with one of these projects!

WONKY-STARS
wall hanging

Imagine this quilt with the blocks set straight—pretty boring, right? Learn how to set any block wonky using the Tall Triangles tool. Yellow and blue is a classic color combination I love to use. Do you have a favorite color combination? Use it to make this quilt.

cutting directions

from	cut	yield
background	five 2½"×42" strips	48—2½" squares
		48 Easy Angle* triangles
blue prints 1-4	one 2½"×42" strips	three 2½" squares
		12 Easy Angle* triangles
blue prints 1-3	two 2½"×42" strips	eleven 2½"×4½" rectangles
blue print 4	one 8"×42" strip	17—1½"×8" sashing rectangles
yellow print	two 6½"×42" strips	48 Tall Triangles**
	one 2½"×42" strip	four 2½" squares
		six 1½" squares
blue print 3	four 2¼"×42" strips	binding

Layer the background and blue-print strips right sides together and cut Easy Angle triangles. They will then be ready to chain sew. If not using an Easy Angle tool, cut 2⅞" squares. Cut once on the diagonal.

**Open and layer both strips right side up. Cut Tall Triangles. No need to trim the "magic angle." If not using the Tall Triangle tool, use template on page 43.*

materials

fabric requirements

blue print 1: ¼ yd.
blue print 2: ¼ yd.
blue print 3: ⅝ yd.
blue print 4: ⅓ yd.
background: ⅜ yd.
yellow print: ½ yd.
backing: 1 yd.
batting: 32"×41"

suggested tools

Easy Angle (EZ Quilting #8823759)
Tall Triangles (EZ Quilting #8823743)

finished dimensions

28½"×37" (8" blocks)

assembling
the blocks

1. Sew all the small triangles together. Press toward the blue fabrics. Assemble 12 blocks as shown, following the pressing arrows. At this point the blocks should measure 6½" square. *(figure 1)*

2. Sew the *diagonal* edge of the yellow Tall Triangles to all sides of the blocks. Center the triangles on the block, as they are longer than needed. Press toward the yellow triangles. Trim evenly on all sides to 8", leaving a ¼" seam allowance at the corners of the star block. *(figure 2)*

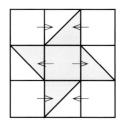

figure 1

assembling
the quilt

1. Sew the blocks together with blue sashing rectangles between them. Make 4 rows of 3 blocks. Press toward the sashing.

2. Sew horizontal sashing rows of 3 blue sashing rectangles and 2 yellow 1½" squares. Press toward the blue sashing. Sew all the rows together, pinning and matching the seam intersections referring to the photo on page 40. Press the seams toward the sashing.

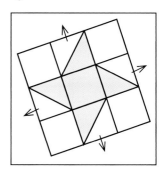

figure 2

borders

1. Sew a variety of seven 2½"×4½" blue rectangles together for the top border. Repeat for the bottom border. Press all one direction. The borders will be longer than needed; trim the ends evenly to fit the quilt top.

2. Sew a variety of nine 2½"×4½" blue rectangles together for the side border. Repeat. Trim the side borders evenly to the length of the quilt top. Sew the 2½" yellow squares to both ends of the side borders. Press toward the yellow squares.

3. Sew the top and bottom borders to the quilt; press toward the borders. Repeat with the side borders. Press toward the borders.

finishing the quilt

1. Trim the batting and backing to 2" larger all around than the quilt top. Layer the backing (wrong-side up), the batting and the quilt top. Baste and quilt as desired.

2. The quilt shown was machine stitched in the ditch between all the blocks as well as inside the blocks and around each star. The pieced border was quilted ¼" from the seams.

binding

1. Sew the 2¼"×42" binding strips together with diagonal seams pressed open. Press the binding in half, wrong sides together, to make a double binding. Sew to the quilt with a ¼" seam, mitering the corners. See pages 119-121 for more instructions on mitering and joining ends.

2. Trim the excess batting and backing, turn the binding to the back side and stitch down by hand with matching thread.

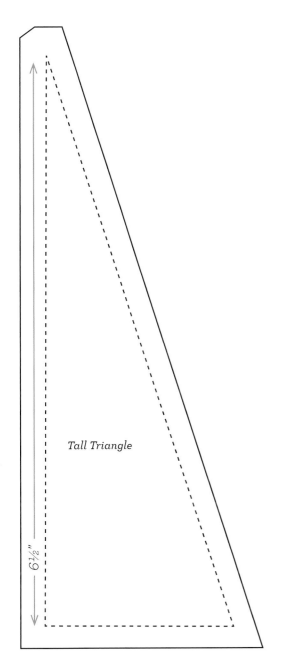

Tall Triangle

6½"

Tall Triangle template

How many projects did you finish last year? This is the perfect time of year to pull out unfinished projects and work on them again. Don't you get a wonderful feeling of accomplishment when you finish something? That said, it's okay to leave some projects unfinished, "resting in pieces" in a closet for a while. When you do return to them, they're "new" again!

Winter is my favorite time of year for quilting. There are no outdoor distractions (play outside in winter in Minnesota? Are you kidding?), and what can be better than cuddling under a quilt you are quilting or binding. With the wonderful Ott Lites we have now, we can easily see to sew after dark. Listen to an audiobook, good music or a favorite old movie while you sew, and you'll double your pleasure.

All the quilters I know give away most of their quilts. Whether you give them away or keep them, don't forget the last step, labeling the quilt. This is your work, so put your name on your creation. It is also important to add the date, the occasion (if there is one) and to whom the gift was presented. You can create your own labels, purchase a printed label or even sign the quilt on the front or back side. Please put your full name on the quilt, not just *Mom*, *Aunt* or *Grandma*—you wouldn't want the wrong mom, aunt or grandma to get the credit for your lovely work!

Below find a recipe for a really good cup of hot chocolate. It makes enough for two, so share with a friend.

recipe

hot chocolate with mint

2 cups milk

2 rounded tbsp. cocoa

4 tsp. sugar

3 tbsp. creme de menthe

whipped cream

chocolate shavings

Whisk first four ingredients together in a small pan. Heat until the milk steams. Pour into mugs; garnish with whipped cream and chocolate shavings. Enjoy!

best friends
SIGNATURE QUILT

Use small-scale, dainty prints and coordinating solids to create the flowers in your own Best Friends Signature Quilt. The center of each "flower" block is perfect for friends' signatures or special quilting designs. Do you know someone who is having a special birthday or who is retiring or moving away? This could be the perfect gift. If needed, make it larger by adding more blocks. The scalloped edge adds the perfect finishing touch.

cutting directions

from	cut	yield
white background	two 2½"×42" strips	48 Easy Angle* triangles
	three 1½"×42" strips	ten 1½"×5½" sashes
		seven 1½"×4½" sashes
yellow solid	one 2½"×42" strip	twelve 2½" squares for block centers
	one 1½"×42" strip	six 1½" squares for cornerstones
solids	one 1½"×12" strip	strip set
each print	one 2½"×21" strip	four Easy Angle* triangles
	one 1½"×12" strip	strip set
six prints	one 1½"×7" strip	four 1½" squares
border fabric	three 4½"×42" strips	borders
	1¼" bias strips for binding	

If not using Easy Angle, cut 2⅞" squares. Cut once on the diagonal for triangles.

Tip: Layer the 2½" white and print strips right sides together to cut the triangles. They will then be ready to chain sew. Also, if you are not using the Easy Scallop tool, mark the intervals along the edge of the border. Find a lid or a plate from your kitchen to mark the curves.

materials

fabric requirements

white background: ⅓ yd.

yellow solid: ⅛ yd.

12 prints for flowers: fat eighths

12 coordinating solids: 2"×12" strips

border and binding: ⅞ yd.

suggested tools

Easy Angle (EZ Quilting #8823759)

*Easy Scallop (EZ Quilting #8823754)

finished dimensions

28"×35" (6" blocks)

*If you don't have the Easy Scallop tool, you can use a lid or a plate from your kitchen to mark and trim a curved edge.

assembling
the blocks

1. Sew the white background and print triangles right sides together on the long edges. Press toward the print fabric. Trim dog-ears. *(figure 1)*

2. Sew the coordinating solid and print 1½"×12" strips together on the long edges. Press toward the print rectangle. Cut the strip set into four 2½" wide units. *(figure 2)*

3. Using the triangle squares from Step 1, the units from Step 2 and a yellow solid square, sew the units together in rows, pressing as directed. *(figure 3)*

4. Sew the rows together, pinning and matching the seams. Make a total of 12 blocks. At this point the blocks should measure 6½" square.

5. Have your friends sign the center of each block.

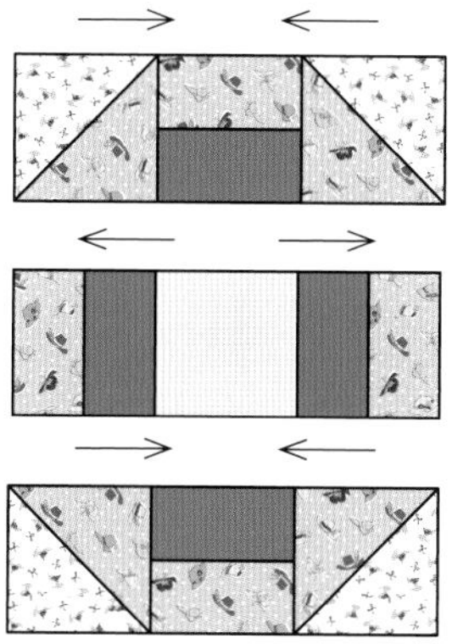

assembling
the quilt

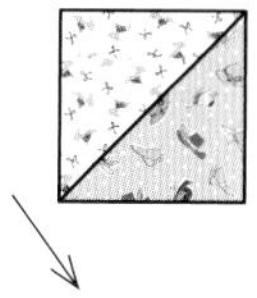

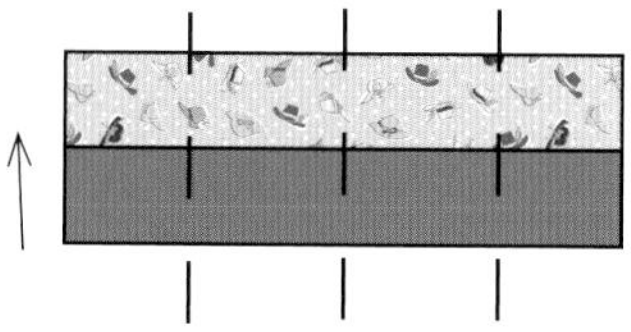

1. Arrange the blocks in 4 rows of 3 blocks. Arrange the short and long sashing strips and cornerstone squares to create the 'small' flowers in the sashing. Once you've determined the arrangement, sew the print squares to the ends of the white background sashing strips, pressing toward the print squares. *(figure 4)*

2. Sew the vertical sashings between the blocks in each row, pressing toward the sashing strips. *(figure 4)*

3. Sew the yellow cornerstones between the horizontal sashing. Press toward the print squares. *(figure 4)*

4. Sew the horizontal sashing rows between the block rows, matching and pinning the seams. Press the seams toward the sashing rows. *(figure 4)*

figure 1   *figure 2*

figure 3

finishing
the quilt

1. Trim a backing that is 2" larger than the quilt top on all sides. Trim the batting to the same size as the backing. Layer the backing (wrong-side up), the batting and the quilt top right-side up. Baste, and then quilt as desired.

2. When the quilting is complete, set the large Easy Scallop tool at 9¼". Mark the center of each of the borders. Starting with the tool at the center on the top border, mark the scallops, with half scallops at the corners as shown. *(figure 5)* Repeat for the bottom border.

3. For the side borders, set the Easy Scallop tool at 8¾". Starting with the tool centered on the, mark scallops. At the corners you will again have half scallops.

4. Do not cut on the marked lines. Hand baste (or machine baste with a walking foot) on the lines to hold the layers together and prevent shifting.

figure 4

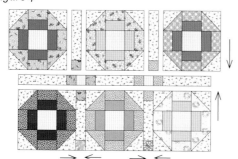

figure 5

binding

1. Cut 1¼" bias-binding strips from the remainder of the border fabric. Join the 1¼" bias-binding lengths with diagonal seams pressed open.

2. Beginning at the top of one scallop, stitch the binding to the quilt using a regular ¼" foot and a ¼" seam allowance. Stitch until you reach the bottom of the *V*, and then stop with the needle down and the presser foot up. Pivot the quilt and the binding around the needle. *(figure 6)*

3. Push any binding behind the needle, lower the presser foot and stitch out of the *V*. *(figure 6)* Continue in this manner around the quilt, mitering the corners of the quilt in the usual way. See pages 119-121 for more instructions on mitering and joining binding ends.

4. Trim the excess batting and backing and then turn the binding under ¼". Turn to the back side and stitch down by hand with matching thread.

figure 6

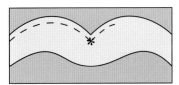

Friendship Quilt

The open centers of the "flower" blocks are the perfect place for your friends to sign their names. Or you may choose to quilt a design in the flower center as I have done. You could easily enlarge the quilt by making more flower blocks.

Friends may move in and out of your life. Some friends we have just for a short time, others for a lifetime. When you think of your good friends, how many of them did you meet through quilting? The hobby we share enriches us through the many friends we make.

The dictionary defines *friendship* as "a term used to denote cooperative and supportive behavior between two or more people." Friends will welcome each other's company and exhibit loyalty toward each other. Their tastes will usually be similar and may converge, and they will share enjoyable activities (such as quilting). They will also engage in mutually helping behavior, such as the exchange of advice and the sharing of hardship (or fabric).

Friendship or signature quilts have a long and interesting history. Permanent ink and a steel-tipped pen were invented in the early 1800s, and signature quilts with inked inscriptions and signatures appeared shortly thereafter. In the early days of our country, there was a great westward movement, and many pioneers packed up their belongings, never to see family and friends again.

Friendship quilts often accompanied these families westward as poignant reminders of those loved ones left behind. Sometimes a woman would collect fabrics, make all the blocks and have loved ones sign them (or someone with nice handwriting would inscribe all the blocks). Or family and friends would make a friendship quilt for someone moving West.

Friendship or signature quilts were often presented to clergymen or important people moving away or in recognition of service. Signature quilts were also used as fund-raisers. Each person would pay a fee to have his or her name put on a quilt to raise money for a worthy project. Often the finished quilt would then be auctioned off to raise even more money.

To show your friends how much you appreciate them, plan a special day of events (but keep it a secret!), set a date and send out invitations. Surprise them with a day filled with special treats— lunch in a tearoom, a visit to some interesting shops, a spa treatment or even a quiet day at your home to sew and talk. Life is partly what we make it and partly what is made by the friends we choose.

sew-easy
BABY QUILT

This pattern really is sew easy! It's great for a beginning quilter or for someone who needs a quick baby gift. The block is simply a square framed with a contrasting color. The "piano key" border is made of rectangles—leftovers from the blocks. This border is very forgiving (if it doesn't fit properly, just take in or let out a few seams) and always coordinates with whatever fabric combinations you are using.

cutting directions

from	cut	yield
yellow print	five 5"×42" strips	ten 5" squares
		56— 2"×5" rectangles
blue print	three 5"×42" strips	ten 5" squares
		28— 2"×5" rectangles
green print	four 5"×42" strips	14—5" squares
	six 2¼"×42" binding strips	26— 2"×5" rectangles
each plaid	seven 2"×42" strips	20—2"×8" rectangles
		20— 2"×5" rectangles

materials

fabric requirements

yellow print: ¾ yd.
blue print: ½ yd.
green print: 1 yd.
yellow plaid: ½ yd.
pink plaid: ½ yd.
green plaid: ½ yd.
backing: 2⅞ yds.
batting: crib size or 51"×60"

finished dimensions

47"×54½" (7 ¾" blocks)

assembling the blocks

1. Sew the 2"×5" green plaid rectangles to 10 yellow 5" squares. Press toward the plaid rectangles. (*figure 1*)

2. Repeat Step 1 with 10 blue squares and yellow plaid rectangles, and 10 green squares with pink plaid rectangles. Press toward the rectangles. (*figure 2*)

3. Sew the matching 2"×8" plaid rectangles to the sides of each of the blocks. Press toward the long rectangles. Make 10 blocks of each color combination. (*figure 3*)

assembling the quilt

1. Arrange the blocks as shown or create your own arrangement. Rotate the blocks so the long rectangle in one block is next to the short rectangle in the adjoining block (no seams to match up!). Press toward the long rectangles. (*figure 4*)

2. Sew together 6 blue, 6 green and 13 yellow rectangles for the top border. Press the seams all one direction. Sew to the top of the quilt. Press toward the quilt. Repeat for the bottom border. (*figure 5*)

3. Sew together 8 blue, 7 green and 15 yellow rectangles for the side border. Make two. Press the seams all one direction. Add green corner squares at both ends of the borders. Press toward the squares. Sew to the sides of the quilt. *Note: The borders can be adjusted as needed by stitching random seams wider or narrower.*

figure 1 *figure 2*

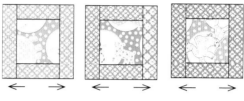

figure 3

figure 4

figure 5

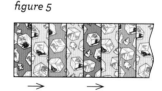

finishing the quilt

1. Layer, baste and quilt as desired. The quilt shown was machine stitched in the ditch around each of the center squares and between each block. The border was stitched in the ditch between the rectangles.

2. Baste a scant ¼" from the edge of the quilt by hand or with a walking foot.

3. Join the binding strips with diagonal seams pressed open. Fold the binding in half, right sides together, and press to make a double binding. Match the raw edges of the binding to the edge of the quilt and stitch the binding in place, mitering the corners. See pages 119-121 for more instructions on mitering and joining the binding ends.

4. Trim the excess batting and backing evenly to ¼". Turn the binding to the back side and stitch down by hand with matching thread.

variation:
sew-easy baby quilt

For a completely different look, bright colors were used to frame a light print featuring owls. Any combination of fabrics will look great in this pattern—give it a try!

cutting directions

from	cut	yield
white print	seven 5"×42" strips	30— 5" squares 56— 2"×5" rectangles
five prints	four 2"×42" strips	12—2"×8" rectangles
	one 5"×42" strip	12 —2"×5" rectangles
yellow daisy	one 5"×42" strip	four 5" squares for corners
	six 2¼"×42" strips	binding

materials

fabric requirements

white print: 1⅛ yds.

green, blue, pink and orange polka dots: ½ yd. each

yellow daisy: 1 yd.

quick-trip
STROLLER QUILT

Just right for the mom and baby on the go! Regular-sized baby quilts may be too large for a stroller or car seat, but this one is just right. No baby? Then sew a just-right blanket for a much loved pet. Don't be put off by all the small squares—this baby utilizes strip sets for easy cutting and piecing.

cutting directions

from each of the fat quarters, cut four 2½"×21" strips.

arrange the colors as shown or devise your own arrangement.

materials

fabric requirements

fat quarters of each:
  1 yellow print
  3 blue prints
  2 green prints
  2 pink prints
  2 lavender prints
green border and
  binding: ⅝ yd.
backing: 1⅛ yd.
batting: 38"×42"

finished dimensions

34"×38" (2" squares)

Signing Baby Quilts

It's always nice to sign your quilts when you finish them. You can make a label (or purchase one) for the back of your quilt and include your full name and who the quilt is made for. Here's a sweet dedication poem you can also add to the label.

Sweet Baby
May you always make wishes
on falling stars,
Believe in fairy tales,
The Tooth Fairy and make-believe.
And may you always have the
faith only a child has.

assembling
the quilt

1. Sew the strips together into 2 different strip sets of 5 colors as shown (or your own arrangement of colors). Press the seams all one direction. Make 4 of each strip set for a total of 8 strip sets. *(figure 1)*

2. Cut a total of sixty-four 2½" wide units. Sew the units together end to end as shown. *(figure 2)*

3. Sew the ends together to make 32 rings. Press these seams the same direction as the other seams. *(figure 3)*

4. Starting in the upper left corner of the quilt, remove 2 adjacent squares on one ring to make the first vertical row. Set aside the squares you have removed. Continue to remove squares from each ring using the diagram as a guide. You will need to re-press the seams in alternate rows to sew them together. Sew two of these sections exactly as shown. They will be the upper left and lower right sections of the quilt. *(figure 4)*

5. For the upper right and lower left sections of the quilt, piece 2 sections of the quilt according to the diagram at the right. *(figure 5)*

6. Using 2 more rings, sew together 2 vertical rows exactly as shown. *(figure 6)* Piece them between the upper 2 sections and the lower 2 sections. Press toward the center.

7. Using 2 more rings, sew together one horizontal row exactly as shown. *(figure 7)* Sew it between the upper and lower sections. Press away from the center.

8. From the green border print, cut four 2½"×42" strips. Measure across the width of the quilt. Trim 2 borders to this length and sew to the top and bottom of the quilt. Press the seams toward the borders. Repeat for the sides of the quilt.

figure 1

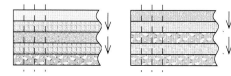

figure 2   *figure 3*

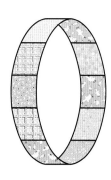

figure 4

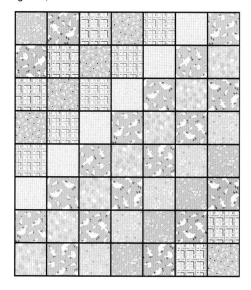

finishing
the quilt

1. Layer the backing (wrong-side up), the batting and the quilt top right-side up. Baste and then quilt as desired.

2. From the green border print, cut four 2¼"×42" strips. Join with diagonal seams pressed open. Press the binding in half, right sides out, to make a double binding.

3. Before binding, hand-baste (or machine-baste using a walking foot) a scant ¼" from the edge of the quilt to hold the layers together.

4. Sew the binding to the quilt with a ¼" seam, mitering the corners and joining the ends according to the directions on pages 119-121.

5. Trim the excess batting and backing. Turn the binding to the back side and stitch down by hand with matching thread. Sign and date!

figure 5

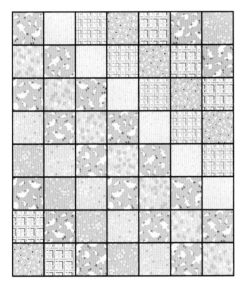

figure 6

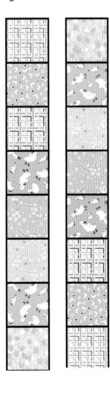

figure 7

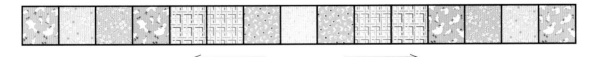

GRAMMY'S
garden

Do you have a green thumb? I don't, but I do try to grow flowers. And in the long winter months in Minnesota, I like to create quilts with flowers. These "flowers" are created with a large hexagon set together in rows with 60-degree triangles—no set-in seams! This project includes a lesson on how to add a flange (the narrow purple inside "border").

For an interesting variation, cut the "flowers" from large-scale prints and offset, them with solid-color contrasting triangles. Can you envision this quilt with black-and-white flowers and red triangles or wildly colored tropical "flowers" and black triangles? Try your own variation of this garden.

cutting directions

from	cut	yield
each print	two 5½"×42" strips	twelve—5½" Hexagons*
yellow solid	nine 3"×42" strips	166—60° Triangles**
	five 2¼"×42" strips	border
	six 2¼" strips	binding
lavender solid	five 1½"×42" strips	flange

*If not using the Hexagon tool, use the template on page 59.
**When cutting the triangles with the 60° Triangle tool, be sure the 3" line is aligned on the edge of the strip. If not using the 60° Triangle tool, use the template below.

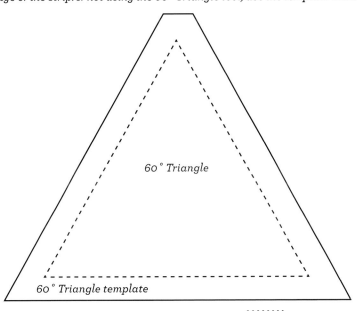

60° Triangle

60° Triangle template

materials

fabric requirements

7 prints: ⅜ yd. of each
yellow solid (includes binding): 1⅝ yds.
lavender solid: ¼ yd.
backing: 2¾ yds.
batting: crib size

suggested tools

60° Triangle (EZ Quilting #882670180)
Hexagon (EZ Quilting #8823754)

finished dimensions

44"×59"

assembling the quilt

1. Sew a yellow triangle to one side of a variety of 10 hexagons, aligning the cut-off tip with the edge of the hexagon for proper placement. *(figure 1)*

2. In the same manner as Step 1, sew yellow triangles on 2 opposite sides of the remainder of the hexagons. Press toward the yellow triangles. *(Tip: Do not trim off the dog-ears on the triangles. They will be very helpful in aligning the seams when you sew the rows together.) (figure 2)*

3. Sew a variety of 7 hexagons with 2 triangles together in a row, pressing as shown. Add an extra yellow triangle at both ends of each row. Make 6 rows. Press toward the left. *(figure 3)*

4. Sew together 6 hexagons with 2 triangles attached, plus 2 hexagons with only 1 triangle to both ends of the row, pressing as shown. Make 5 rows. Press toward the right. *(figure 4)*

5. Sew the Steps 3 and 4 rows together, alternating the rows. Press the seams all one direction.

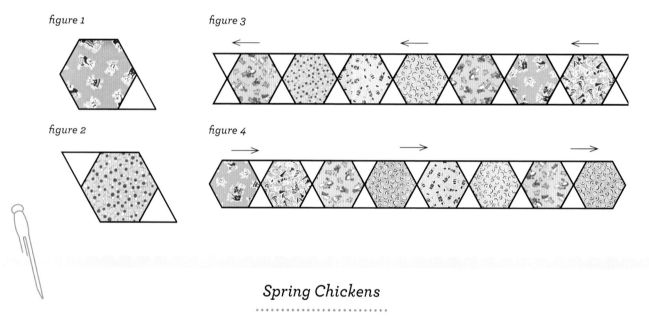

figure 1

figure 2

figure 3

figure 4

Spring Chickens

Spring is finally coming to Minnesota after a very long, cold, snowy winter. Naturally as we get closer to spring, my thoughts turn to flowers, gardening and, strangely enough, baby chicks! Have I mentioned I grew up on a farm? Every spring my mother ordered baby chicks, and we were always so excited to see the fluffy yellow chicks. Visiting them in their warm brooder house was a treat. We had to be very quiet and move slowly so as not to startle them. If startled, the chicks would run to a corner and pile up on each other, and some would be smothered. They were so adorable in their fluffy yellow down, but before too long the white feathers would sprout. At that stage they resembled gawky teenagers.

In the past, most farm women and a few women in town raised chickens. It was usually the housewife's job—and income. Both eggs and chickens were a source of food for the family, but the eggs could be sold for a bit of money every week. Many housewives used their "egg money" to purchase fabric and supplies for making their quilts. When chicken feed was sold in colorful cloth bags (feedsacks), that was also a source of free fabric for the housewife. Most of the feedsacks we find today once held chicken feed—so it's no wonder feedsacks have been called "chicken linen."

When we purchased our home, the backyard held a small horse barn and a chicken coop with fencing. Apparently the woman who lived there once raised chickens in the backyard. Since that time, most cities and towns have passed regulations about raising farm animals, but a new movement is underfoot to bring chickens to backyards everywhere. New York City, Los Angeles, Portland and Seattle all permit urban chickens now. Such cities generally limit residents to five or fewer hens, with no roosters (too noisy).

While dreaming of gardening and spring flowers (and chickens in the backyard), enjoy sewing the *Grammy's Garden* quilt.

adding the borders

1. At this point you can trim the side edges even, leaving a ¼" seam allowance. Or, if you prefer the look of the zigzag edges, remove one yellow triangle at each corner of the quilt. To bind this irregular edge, you'll need to pivot at the inner corners as on a scalloped edge and miter the outer corners. See page 119 for instructions.

2. To add a flange as shown, fold 2 of the 1½"×42" solid lavender strips in half, wrong sides together, and press to make the flange. Measure, trim and baste (with a long stitch and a scant ¼" seam allowance) the flange to the top and bottom of the quilt. Piece the remaining 3 lavender strips with diagonal seams pressed open. Measure, trim and baste the flange to sides of the quilt.

3. In the same manner, measure, trim and sew the 2¼"×42" yellow borders to the top and bottom of the quilt. Piece the remaining yellow borders strips; measure, trim and sew the border to the sides of the quilt top.

finishing the quilt

1. Layer, baste and quilt as desired.

2. Sew the binding strips together with diagonal seams pressed open. Fold the binding and press in half, wrong sides together.

3. Sew to the quilt with a ¼" seam, mitering the corners. See pages 119-121 for instructions on mitering and joining binding ends.

4. Trim the excess batting and backing, and stitch the binding down by hand with matching thread.

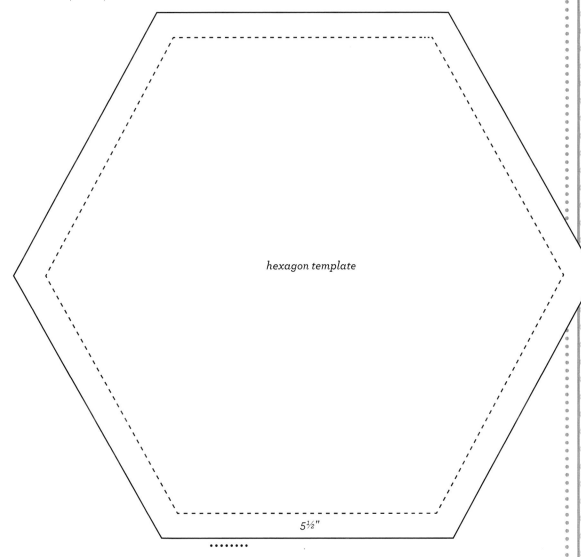

hexagon template

5½"

SIMPLY CRAZY
quilt

My *Simply Crazy Quilt* utilizes cotton fabric in irregular shapes. In making this quilt, you will learn an easy way to cut and sew those irregular shapes. The embroidery, embellishment and quilting are optional. The "real" crazy quilts were never quilted, just tacked to the backing in a few places.

cutting directions

Using the Simply Crazy* tool and any of the fabrics, cut 16 centers. The centers can be all one size or a variety of sizes. Cut as shown. *(figure 1)*

Cut the fat quarters in half to make two 9"×21" rectangles. Cut uneven wedge-shaped pieces from those rectangles as shown. *(figure 2)*

Cut the stabilizer into 16—10½" squares.

If not using the Simply Crazy tool, use template on page 64.

figure 1

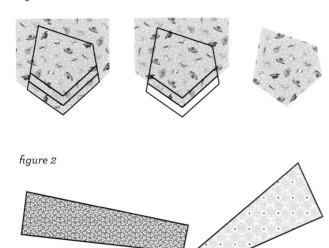

figure 2

materials

fabric requirements

fat quarters of 10 fabrics:
- 1 yellow print
- 2 blue prints
- 2 green prints
- 3 red prints
- 1 lavender print
- 1 orange print

blue border/binding: 1⅛ yds.

backing: 3 yds.

suggested tools

Simply Crazy (EZ Quilting #8823746)

additional supplies

batting (optional):
- twin size
- stabilizer: 5 yds.
- embroidery floss, trims (optional)

finished dimensions

46½"×56½" (10" blocks)

assembling the blocks

1. Place a center in the middle of one square of stabilizer. Choose a wedge-shaped piece, put it right sides together with the center and sew a ¼" seam. *(figure 3)*

2. Fold the stabilizer out of the way and trim off the excess fabric on both edges. *(figure 4)*

3. Working in a clockwise or counterclockwise manner, continue adding strips and then pressing and trimming. *(figure 5 and 6)*

4. When all the stabilizer is covered, trim the edges evenly to 10½". Repeat to make a total of 16 blocks. *(figure 7)*

5. Embroidery can be added to the block at this point.

assembling the quilt

1. Sew the blocks together in 4 rows of 4 blocks, pressing the seams in opposite directions in alternating rows.

2. Sew the rows together, pinning and matching the seams.

3. If you choose, you can add embroidery over the joining seams.

4. Cut six 3½"×42" blue border strips. Measure the width of the quilt. Trim 2 borders to this length and sew to the top and bottom of the quilt. Press toward the borders.

5. Measure the quilt through the length. Piece and trim 2 borders to this length. Sew to the sides of the quilt. Press toward the borders just added.

figure 3

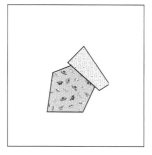

figure 4

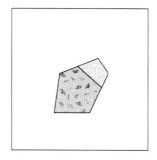

figure 7

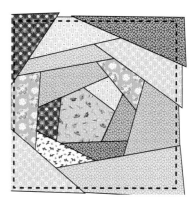

figure 5

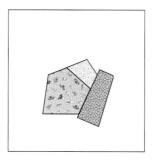

figure 6

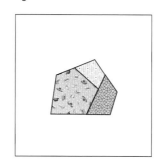

Continue to page 64»

Quilting and food just seem to go hand in hand, don't you think? Here's a good soup recipe to make on a cold, dreary day. Put all the ingredients in a slow cooker and spend the day sewing. Serve with warm corn bread, and you have a hearty, healthy meal!

recipe

chicken enchilada soup (for slow cooker)

1½ lbs. of chicken breast, cubed and browned

one 46 oz. can of V8 juice

2 cans black beans, drained

1 bag frozen corn

½ cup celery, diced

1 jar salsa, mild

Put all in the ingredients in a slow cooker for four to five hours on high. Serve with a dollop of sour cream and shredded mozzarella cheese.

finishing the quilt

1. Piece a backing that is at least 5" larger than the quilt top. Batting is optional for a crazy quilt.

2. Layer the backing wrong-side up, batting if desired, and the quilt top right-side up. The crazy quilt can then be tied from the front or back (traditional method), or it can be quilted—your preference!

3. Cut six 2¼" strips of blue print for binding. Join the ends with diagonal seams pressed open. Fold the binding in half, wrong sides together, and press.

4. Sew the binding to the quilt with a ¼" seam, mitering the corners. See pages 119-121 for more instructions on mitering and joining the ends. Trim the excess batting and backing, turn the binding to the back side and stitch down by hand with matching thread.

Simply Crazy template

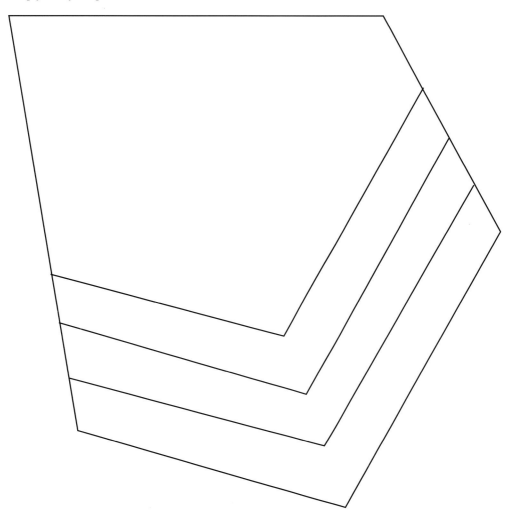

variation:
simply crazy quilt
(27½" square)

Any combination of fabrics will look great
in this pattern—give it a try!

From the fat eighths, cut:
Four centers any size using the Simply Crazy tool
Four 4¼" matching squares for border corners
The remainder of the fat eighths into wedge-shaped pieces

Assemble the blocks as in the larger pattern.

Sew the 4 blocks together into a square.
Cut two 4¼"×42" strips of border fabric. Sew borders to the
quilt, adding the corner squares.
Cut three 2¼"×42" strips for binding.

materials

fabric requirements

9 fat eighths (9"×21")
border: ¼ yd.
binding: ¼ yd.
backing: ⅞ yd.
batting: 30" square
stabilizer: four 10½" squares

chapter

3

Full-Size Quilts

In this group of quilts you will find both very easy quilts (*Picnic Quilt*) and more challenging quilts (*Butterfly Garden*). If you don't enjoy hand- or machine- quilting, you could make the *Home Sweet Home* or the *Blue-Ribbon Winner* tablecloths. Just for fun (and to learn a new technique), try *Milady's Fans. Garden Sunshine, Laundry-Basket Quilt* and *Tiptoe Through the Flowers* are great scrappy quilts if you have a few "leftovers." Nothing is more satisfying than making a large quilt.

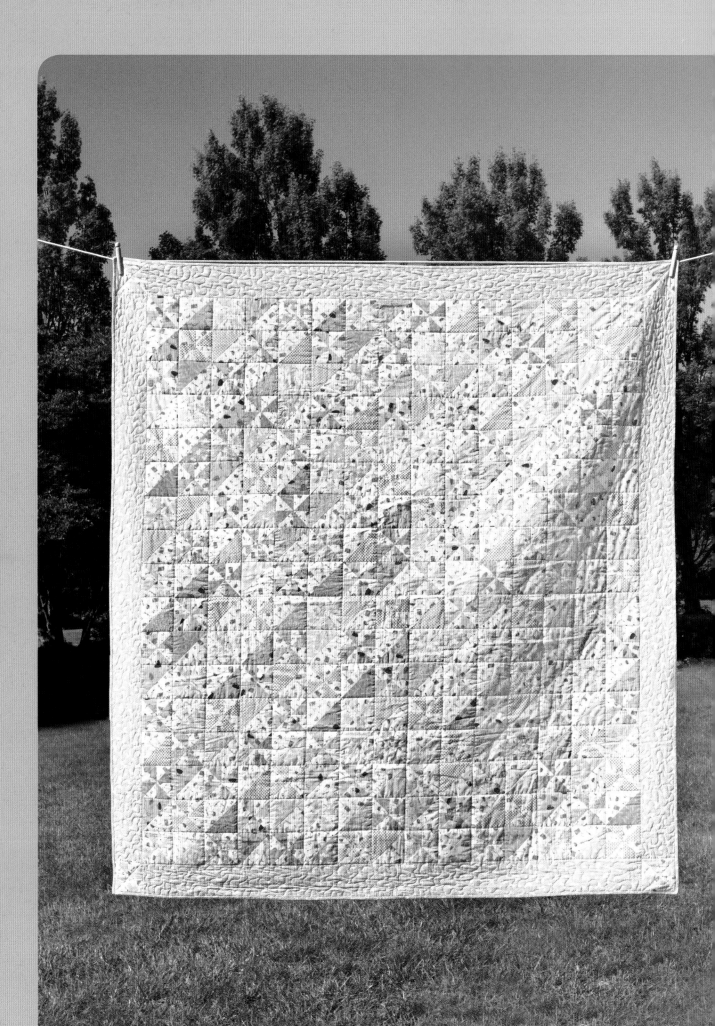

HOME SWEET
home

Do you have scraps or leftovers from other projects? This is the perfect scrap quilt or tablecloth. There are only small and large triangles in the quilt, and the more fabrics you mix in, the better! Any combination of fabrics will work, as long as you divide the fabrics into lights and darks. If it's a tablecloth, no quilting is necessary, although I do back the tablecloth and finish the edges. I also add in a bit of stitching in the ditch to hold the two layers together. Or make it into a quilt with a thin batting so it can be used for a tablecloth or a lightweight summer quilt.

cutting directions

from	cut	yield
each light print	three 4½"×42" strips	44 Easy Angle* triangles
	seven 2½"×42" strips	176 Easy Angle* triangles
each dark print	one 4½"×42" strip	Twelve Easy Angle* triangles
	two 2½"×42" strips	48 Easy Angle* triangles
border fabric	seven 4½"×42" strips	border
binding fabric	2¼" wide bias strips or eight 2¼"×42" strips	at least 300" of binding

If not using the Easy Angle tool, cut 2⅞" and 4⅞" squares respectively. Cut once on the diagonal.

Tip: Layer the same size light and dark strips right sides together and cut with Easy Angle. They are then ready to chain sew.

materials

fabric requirements

3 light prints: 1 yd. each
11 dark prints: ⅓ yd. each
border: 1 yd.
binding (optional): ⅔ yd.
backing (optional): 4⅛ yds.
batting (optional): twin size

suggested tools

Easy Angle (EZ Quilting #88223759)

finished dimensions

68"×76" (4" blocks)

assembling the half-square triangles

1. Sew all the large light and dark triangles together on the diagonal edge. Trim dog-ears. Press toward the darkest fabric. You should have 132 half-square triangles measuring 4½" square. (*figure 1*)

2. Sew the small light and dark triangles together on the diagonal edge. Trim dog-ears. You should have 528 half-square triangles measuring 2½" square. (*figure 2*)

3. Sew matching units from Step 2 together in pairs. Press the seams as shown. Make 24 pairs from each fabric. (*figure 3*)

4. Using matching units from Step 3, sew 2 pairs together to make 12 pinwheel blocks from each dark print. Twist the center seam to open (see page 117). The seams should now spin around the center. Press. At this point you should have a total of 132 blocks that measure 4½" square. (*figure 4*)

5. Alternating pinwheel blocks from Step 4 and large half-square triangles from Step 1, sew 15 units together as shown. Press toward the half-square triangles. Make 9 rows. (*figure 5*)

6. Sew large half-square triangles and pinwheel blocks together in rows as shown, pressing toward the half-square triangles. Make 8 rows. (*figure 6*)

7. Sew the rows together, matching seams and alternating Step 5 and 6 rows. Press the seams all one direction.

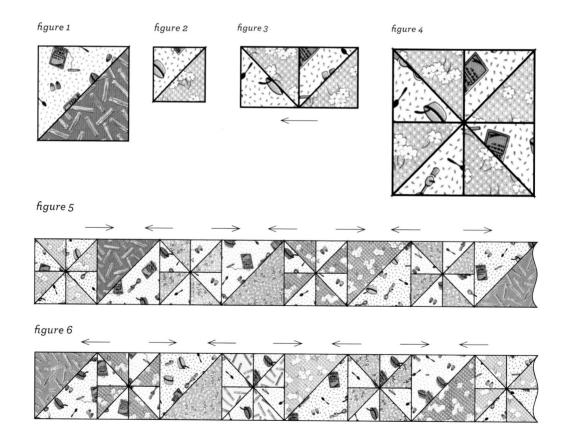

figure 1

figure 2

figure 3

figure 4

figure 5

figure 6

finishing the tablecloth

1. Piece the 4½" wide border strips together. Measure the width of the quilt. Trim two borders to this length. Measure the length of the quilt. Trim two borders to this length. Set aside.

2. Sew the top and bottom borders to the quilt. Press toward the borders. Add pinwheel blocks to both ends of the side borders. Press toward the borders. Sew the borders to the sides of the quilt. Press toward the borders.

3. You can turn the edges under a scant ¼" twice to hem and use as a tablecloth. Or layer with backing and batting and quilt as desired. The tablecloth shown was machine quilted in the ditch between each of the blocks, and a meander was stitched in the border.

4. If you have chosen to quilt the tablecloth/quilt, bind with 2¼" double binding joined with diagonal seams pressed open. Miter the corners. See pages 119-121 for more instructions on mitering corners and joining binding ends.

5. Trim the excess batting and backing, turn the binding to the back side and stitch down with matching thread.

History of Tablecloths

Our mothers and grandmothers used tablecloths instead of place mats, and in their day it was a matter of pride to have a well-stocked linen closet. Washing and ironing and keeping the linens stain-free was quite a chore in the days before automatic washers and dryers!

The 1940s and '50s era is well known for its colorful tablecloths splashed with big flowers or fruit. Each of the states was also represented on those colorful tablecloths, which are highly collectible, as are all well-preserved tablecloths from any era. Smaller square tablecloths were meant for use on the new "card tables," often sporting a motif of hearts, diamonds, spades and clubs for the ladies' bridge-club parties. You can still find nice examples of vintage tablecloths in antiques stores, flea markets, estate sales and on Ebay.

GARDEN
sunshine

The flowers on this quilt remind me of bachelor's button flowers. Did you know "bachelor button" is a euphemism for safety pin? Supposedly a bachelor wouldn't know how to sew on a button and would substitute a safety pin instead. Do you have an old-fashioned button box for all sorts of fancy buttons? I have several containers full, and had a great time searching out the colorful plastic buttons from the 1930s era for my *Garden Sunshine* quilt. If you aren't so lucky to have inherited a button box, very nice reproduction buttons are available.

cutting directions

from	cut	yield
background print	eleven 3½"×42" strips	168 pairs of Recs* triangles
each fat quarter	two 3½"×21" strips	twelve Tri* triangles
	one 5"×21" strip	ten 2"×5" rectangles
one blue fat quarter	one 5"×21" strip	four 5"×5" squares for corners
variety of prints		30—2"×2" squares for cornerstones
yellow solid	twelve 2"×42" strips	71—2"×6½" rectangles for sashing
	five 2"×42" strips	inner border
	seven 2¼"×42" strips	binding

Be sure to accurately trim off the small corner on the Recs triangles, the "magic angle." This is your placement guide for sewing. If not using the Tri-Recs tool, use the Tri template on page 74 and the Recs template on page 75.

materials

fabric requirements

background: 1¼ yds.

prints for flowers: 14 fat quarters

yellow solid for sashing, inner border and binding: 1½ yds.

backing: 3½ yds.

batting: twin size

suggested tools

Tri-Recs (EZ Quilting #8823753)

additional requirements

buttons for centers of flowers (optional)

finished dimensions

56"×63½" (6" blocks)

assembling the flower blocks

Note: Sew an exact ¼" seam allowance, or the units won't be square when finished.

1. Using a pair of Recs triangles, sew to a Tri triangle as shown. *(figure 1)* Press toward the Recs triangles. Repeat for all the Tri-Recs units. They should measure 3½" at this point. *(figure 2)*

2. Sew matching Tri-Recs units together in pairs as shown. Press as shown. *(figure 3)*

3. Sew matching pairs together to make a flower block. Twist the center seam to open *(see page 117)*. Make a total of 42 flower blocks. At this point the blocks should measure 6½" square. *(figure 4)*

assembling the quilt

1. Arrange the blocks in 7 rows of 6 blocks. Sew yellow sashing strips between the blocks in each row. Press toward the sashing strips.

2. Assemble 6 horizontal sashing rows of 6 yellow sashes and 5 print cornerstones. Press toward the sashing strips.

3. Sew the block rows and horizontal sashing rows together, pressing toward the sashing rows.

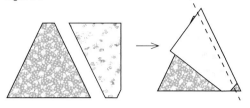

figure 1

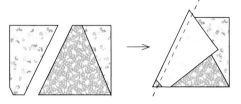

figure 2

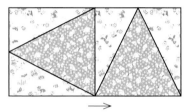

figure 3

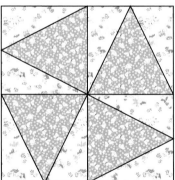

figure 4

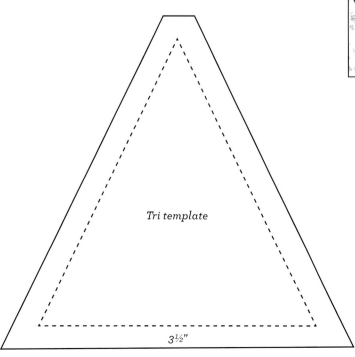

Tri template

3½"

adding the borders

1. Piece, measure and trim 2 yellow solid borders the width of the quilt. Sew to the top and bottom of the quilt. Refer to photo on page 72 for arrangement. Press toward the borders.

2. Repeat for the sides of the quilt.

3. Using the print 2"×5" rectangles, sew 31 together on the long edges to make the top and bottom borders. Press the seams all one direction. Sew to the top and bottom of the quilt. Press the seams toward the inner border. (*Tip: If the borders don't quite fit, sew a few random seams narrower or wider until they fit.*)

4. Sew 36 print rectangles together on the long edges. Make 2 side borders. Press the seams all one direction. Add the cornerstones at both ends of the side borders. Press toward the cornerstones. Sew to the sides of the quilt. Press the seams toward the inner border.

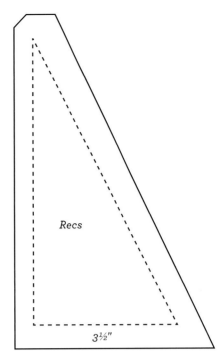

Recs

3½"

Recs template

finishing the quilt

1. Piece a backing that is at least 4" larger than your quilt top. Layer the backing (wrong-side up), the batting and the quilt top (right-side up). Baste together and then quilt as desired.

2. Before binding, hand- or machine-baste (using a walking foot) a scant ¼" from the edge of your quilt to hold the layers together.

3. To bind, sew the 2¼"×42" yellow solid strips together with diagonal seams pressed open. Fold the binding in half, wrong sides together, and press to make a double binding. Sew to the quilt with a ¼" seam, mitering the corners. See pages 119-121 for more instructions on mitering and joining the binding ends.

4. Trim the excess batting and backing, turn the binding to the wrong side and stitch down by hand with matching thread.

embellishment

If desired, sew a vintage (or new!) button in the center of each flower.

BUTTERFLY
garden

This quilt uses the same four-patch flower block as in *Garden Sunshine*, but in this quilt it is combined with appliquéd butterflies. Learn some appliqué techniques, add a touch of embroidery to the butterflies and sew the butterfly blocks together with flower blocks to make an extra-special quilt.

cutting directions for butterfly blocks

from	cut
twelve different fat quarters	one pair wings (see page 81)
coordinating solids	lower pairs of wings (see page 81)
brown solid	twelve bodies (see page 81)
background print	four 13"×42" strips
	cut strips into twelve 13" squares

appliqué directions

(refer to page 122 for instructions)

Using fusible web or the freezer-paper method, appliqué the butterfly wings and bodies to the background squares, setting the butterflies on the diagonal of the blocks. Buttonhole stitch if desired, and add the antennae with two strands of embroidery floss. After the blocks are completed, press and trim to exactly 12½" square.

materials

fabric requirements

white background: 2½ yds.

prints for butterflies, flowers and triangles: 17 fat quarters

inner border, binding and wings (pink solid): 1 yd.

outer border: 2⅜ yds.

solids for butterflies: fat eighths of brown, dark blue, dark green, orange, lavender

backing: 5 yds.

suggested tools

Tri-Recs (EZ Quilting #8823753)

Companion Angle (EZ Quilting #882670139)

*Easy Scallop (EZ Quilting #8823754)

additional requirements

black embroidery floss or #8 perle cotton

fusible web or freezer paper: 3 yds.

finished dimensions

67"×84" (12½" blocks)

If you don't have the Easy Scallop tool, you can use a lid or a plate from your kitchen to mark and trim a curved edge.

cutting directions for flowers and setting triangles

from	cut	yield
background fabric	nine 3½"×42" strips	136 pairs of Recs* triangles
each fat quarter	one 5"×21" strip	two Companion Angle** triangles
	one 3½"×21" strip	eight Tri* triangles

Please see pages 74-75 for the Tri and Rec templates if not using the tools.
**If not using the Companion Angle tool, cut one 10¼" square. Cut twice on the diagonal like an X. You will only need two of the triangles.*

flower blocks

Note: Sew an exact ¼" seam allowance, or the units won't be square when finished.

1. Assemble all your Tri-Recs units using the print Tri shapes and the background Recs shapes. Press the seams as shown. Make a total of 136 units. At this point, the units should measure 3½". (figures 1 and 2)

2. Using 4 matching Tri-Recs units, sew them together in pairs as shown. Press as shown. (figure 3)

3. Sew the pairs together to make a flower block. Twist the center seam to open (see page 117). Press the seams all one direction around the center. Make a total of 34 flower blocks. At this point, the blocks should measure 6½" square. (figure 4)

4. Sew 4 flower blocks together to make a large 12½" square flower block. Make six large flower blocks. The remaining 10 flower blocks are used in the setting triangles.

setting triangles

1. Sew 2 different print triangles to adjacent sides of the remainder of the flower blocks as shown. Press toward the triangles. Note that the triangles are slightly larger than needed. Make ten setting triangle units. (figure 5)

2. Using 8 print triangles (there will be some triangles left over), sew them together in pairs to create 4 large corner triangles. Press the seams open. (figure 6)

figure 1

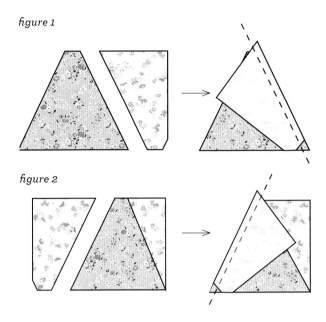

figure 2

figure 3

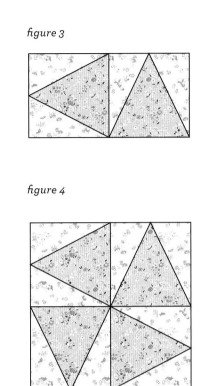

figure 4

figure 5

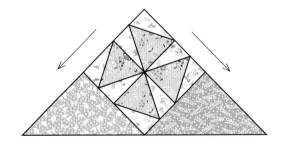

figure 6

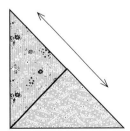

assembling the quilt

1. Arrange the butterfly blocks, the large flower blocks and the pieced setting triangles in diagonal rows as shown. *(figure 7)*

2. Sew the blocks together, pressing the seams toward the butterfly blocks and the setting triangles.

3. Sew the rows together, pinning and matching seams.

4. Press the row seams all one direction. When finished, trim the edges even, leaving at least a ¼" seam allowance from the corners of the blocks.

inner borders

1. Cut six 1½"×42" pink inner border strips.

2. Sew the 1½" pink border strips together with diagonal seams pressed open.

3. Measure and trim 2 borders the width of the quilt. Sew to the top and bottom of the quilt. Press toward the borders.

4. Measure the width of the quilt and trim 2 borders to this length. Sew to the sides of the quilt. Press toward the borders.

outer borders

1. Cut 4 borders 7" wide by the length of the fabric. Cut the outer border strips *lengthwise* to avoid piecing them.

2. Trim 2 borders the width of the quilt. Sew to the top and bottom of the quilt and press toward the borders.

3. Trim the remaining 2 borders the length of the quilt. Sew to the sides of the quilt. Press toward the borders.

figure 7

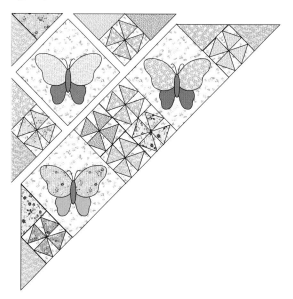

finishing the quilt

1. Quilting: Piece a backing that is 4" larger all around than the top of the quilt. Layer the backing (wrong-side up), the batting and then the quilt top (right-side up). Baste and quilt as desired. The quilt shown was machine meandered in the background areas, and the lines were stitched in the butterfly wings. An all-over design was quilted in the border.

2. Marking Scallops: Set the Easy Scallop tool at 8". Mark scallops along the edge of the quilt, aligning them with the setting triangles and leaving the corners square. Baste by hand (or with a walking foot on the machine) on the marked scallop line, but do not cut on that line!

3. Binding: Cut the remainder of the pink solid fabric into 1¼" wide bias strips. Join the strips with diagonal seams pressed open. Stitch the binding in place with a ¼" seam (and using the ¼" foot) using the marked line as a placement guide for the binding. When you get to the bottom of the *V*, stop with the needle down and pivot around that point. Align the binding, pushing any pleats that form behind the needle. Resume stitching. Trim the excess batting and backing off evenly to ¼". No need to clip in the *V*s. Turn the binding under and stitch down by hand on the back side of the quilt, covering the line of stitching. A small pleat will form in the *V*. See pages 120-122 for more information on binding a scalloped edge and joining binding ends. Sign and date!

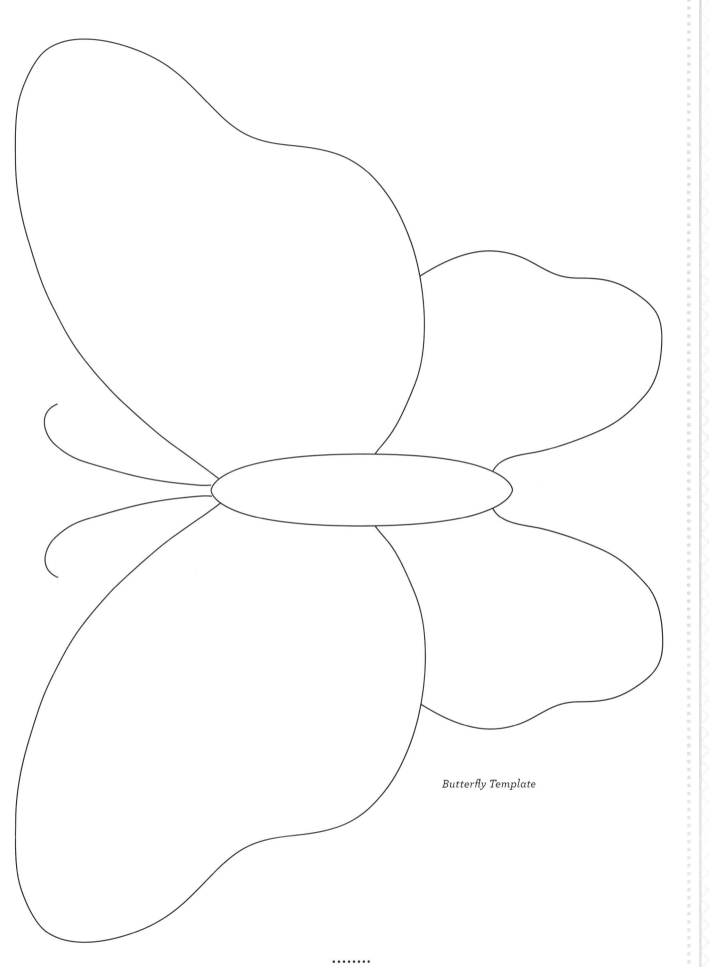

Butterfly Template

STARS FOR
mama

What a bright, happy quilt! Make this up in any combination of fabrics for a lovely wall hanging or use it as a tablecloth. The small stars are the same block (different size) as the large stars and are actually pieced into the sashing.

cutting the large stars

from	cut	yield
background print	four 2½"×42" strips	64—2½" squares
	five 2½"×42" strips	64 Companion Angle* triangles*
each fat quarter	two 4½"×4½" squares	
	two 2½"×21" strips	16 Easy Angle** triangles

If you are not using Companion Angle, cut 16 squares 5¼"×5¼". Cut twice on the diagonal like an X.
**If you are not using Easy Angle, cut eight 2⁷⁄₈" squares from each fat quarter. Cut once on the diagonal.*

cutting the sashing and small stars

from	cut	yield
background print	six 2½"×42" strips	24—2½"×8½" sashing rectangles
seven fat quarters	one 2½"×2½" square	eight 1½"×1½" squares
one fat quarter	two 2½"×2½" squares	16—1½"×1½" squares

materials

fabric requirements

assorted prints: 8 fat quarters
background: 2¼ yds.
binding: ½ yd.
backing: 3¼ yds.

suggested tools

Easy Angle (EZ Quilting #8823759)
Companion Angle (EZ Quilting #882670139)

finished dimensions

50 ½"×50 ½" (8 ½" blocks)

cutting the borders

from	cut	yield
background print	four 2½"×42" strips	2½"×42" nine strips for inner and outer borders
		80 Easy Angle* triangles
		2½"×2½" eight squares
each fat quarter	one 2½"×21" strip	ten Easy Angle* triangles
binding fabric	six 2¼"×42" strips	binding

Tip: Layer the 2½" print and background strips right sides together and cut Easy Angle triangles. They are then ready to chain sew.

If not using Easy Angle, cut 2⅞" squares; cut once on the diagonal.

assembling the large stars

1. Sew a small print triangle to the right edge of the background triangle. Press toward the print triangle. Repeat on the adjacent edge. Press. Make 64 of these "flying geese" units. The units should measure 2½"×4½". (*figure 1*)

2. Sew matching flying-geese units to opposite sides of a 4½"×4½" print square. Press toward the square. Repeat for each of the large squares. Make 16. (*figure 2*)

3. Sew background squares to both ends of the remaining flying-geese units. Press toward the squares. (*figure 3*)

4. Sew the Step 3 units to the sides of the Step 2 units, making 16 star blocks. Press toward the centers. At this point the blocks should measure 8½" square. (*figure 4*)

figure 1

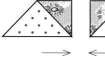

figure 2

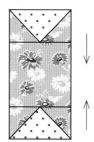

figure 3

figure 4

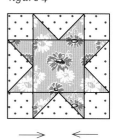

assembling the sashing
and small stars

1. Arrange the star blocks in four rows of four blocks, with background sashing rectangles between the blocks, referring to the quilt image for layout. Do not sew together yet.

2. Sew matching 1½" print squares to the corners of the sashing rectangles to make the small star points. To do this, mark a diagonal line on the wrong side of the small squares. Align the square in one corner of a sashing rectangle, right sides together. (*figure 5*) Stitch on the marked line, trim seam allowance to ¼" and press. Repeat with matching fabric on the nearest adjacent corner. (*figure 6*) Match the star point prints to the star center square print.

3. Twelve sashing rows will need to be double ended. Repeat Step 2 for the other side of those sashing rows. Make sure these star points match star cornerstones before sewing.

4. Sew the blocks and sashing together in rows. Press the seams toward the sashing. Sew the rows together, pressing toward the sashing rows.

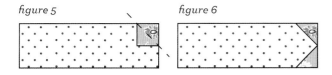

figure 5   figure 6

adding the borders

1. Measure, piece and sew 2½" wide inner background print borders to the quilt top. Press.

2. Sew each background triangle to a fat quarter triangle along the long side to make 80 squares. Sew four units of ten triangle squares pointing right, and four units of ten triangle squares pointing left. Join a right and a left unit with a background square between them. Press. Sew pieced borders to the top and bottom of the quilt. Press. Add background squares to the ends of the remaining pieced borders and sew to the sides of the quilt. Press. (*Tip: If the pieced border is too small, trim the quilt evenly to fit the pieced border.*)

3. Measure, piece and sew 2½" wide outer-background print borders to the quilt top. Press.

finishing the quilt

1. Layer the backing wrong-side up, the batting and the quilt top right-side up. Baste, then quilt as desired.

2. Join the binding strips with diagonal seams pressed open. Press in half, right sides out, for a double binding. Bind with 2¼" double binding stitched with a ¼" seam, mitering the corners. See pages 119-121 for instructions on mitering corners and joining the ends.

3. Trim the excess batting and backing. Turn the binding to the back side and stitch down by hand with matching thread.

recipe

mom's apple pie to end all apple pies

Peel, core, and slice four to five apples (or enough to fill a large pie pan).

Toss with:

⅓ cup sugar

⅓ cup brown sugar

1 tsp. cinnamon

3 tbsp. flour

Topping:

½ cup flour

½ tsp. cinnamon

¼ cup brown sugar

¼ cup butter

Fill a 9" unbaked pie shell with the coated apples. Using a pastry blender or a fork, cut butter into flour-sugar-cinnamon mixture. Scatter over the apple filling. Bake at 350° F for 45 minutes or until top is nicely browned and apples are tender. (Baking time depends upon type of apples, how high you mound the pie and the type of pie pan used.)

laundry-basket
QUILT

Baskets have long been a favorite motif of quilters, and this particular block is generally known as "cake stands." This quilt could be a great scrappy project—the basket tops could all be different with coordinating solid baskets. Using the same fabric for the setting triangles as for the border creates an interesting frame for the basket blocks.

cutting directions

from	cut	yield
background fabric	seven 2"×42" strips	200 Easy Angle* triangles
	three 2"×42" strips	50—2" squares
	two 2½"×42" strips	50 Easy Angle* triangles
	four 4"×42" strips	100—1½"×4" rectangles
each print	one 3½"×21" strip	five Easy Angle* triangles
	two 2"×21" strips	20 Easy Angle* triangles
blue solid	three 3½"×42" strips	50 Easy Angle* triangles
	three 1½"×42" strips	100 Easy Angle* triangles
	five 1½"×42" strips	inner border
	six 2¼"×42" strips	binding
border print	three 4½"×42" strips	18 Companion Angle** triangles
	one 5½"×42" strip	two 5½" squares, cut once on the diagonal for corner squares
	five 3½"×42" strips	outer border

*If not using the Easy Angle tool, cut 2³/₈" or 3⁷/₈" squares respectively. Cut once on the diagonal.
**If not using the Companion Angle tool, cut 9¼" squares. Cut twice on the diagonal like an X.

materials

fabric requirements

prints: 10 fat eighths
background: 1¼ yds.
blue solid: 1⅛ yds.
border: 1⅛ yds.
backing: 3 yds.
batting: 54"×62"

suggested tools

Easy Angle (EZ Quilting #8823759)

Companion Angle (EZ Quilting #882670139)

finished dimensions

47"×55½"

assembling
the quilt

1. Sew all the small print and background triangles together on the diagonal edge. Trim the dog-ears. *(figure 1)*

2. Sew the Step 1 units together into *A* and *B* pairs as shown. Add background squares to the *B* pairs. *(figure 2)* Make 5 of each for each print.

3. Sew the large-print and solid-colored triangles together. Trim the dog-ears. *(figure 3)*

4. Sew the Step 2 *a* pairs to the large triangle-squares as shown. *(figure 4)*

5. Sew the Step 2 *B* pairs to the adjacent side of the Step 4 unit. *(figure 5)*

6. Sew half of the small solid-colored triangles to the ends of the 1½"×4" background rectangles. Repeat with the remaining triangles, but have them facing the opposite direction as shown. Make 50 of each. *(Tip: It doesn't matter where the cut-off tip is placed.) (figure 6)*

7. Sew one each of the Step 6 units to adjacent sides of the Step 5 units. Trim the dog-ears. *(figure 7)*

8. Sew the 2½" background triangle to the bottom of the basket. Make a total of 50 basket blocks. At this point the blocks should measure 6" squares. *(figure 8)*

Instructions continued on page 90»

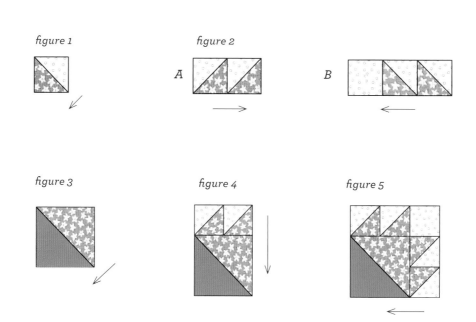

figure 1

figure 2

A

B

figure 3

figure 4

figure 5

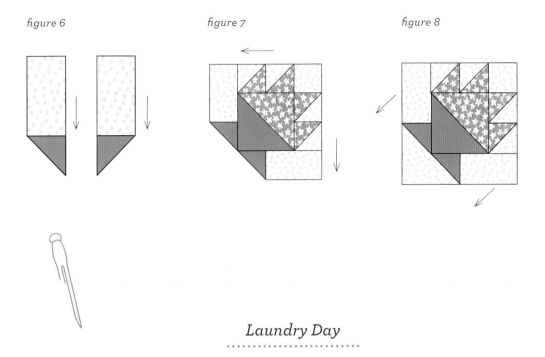

figure 6   figure 7   figure 8

Laundry Day

With our modern washers and dryers, we don't need to spend much time or effort doing laundry. It's simply a chore we fit in our day. That was not the case, however, for our mothers and grandmothers. Wash day was an all-day job, with the ironing saved for the next day!

Wash day was usually on a Monday. Before there were hot-water heaters in every home, water had to be heated on the wood-burning stove in great kettles. And if you didn't have the luxury of running water, the water first had to be carried into the house.

After the water was heated, homemade lye soap would be shaved or grated into the hot water in the washtub to dissolve. If you were lucky to have an "automatic" wash machine, the machine would do the agitating, and you could run the clothes through the wringer (watch your fingers!). If you weren't so lucky, a washboard was used, and you had to wring out the clothes by hand (no doubt leading to very sore hands by the end of the day). All the white clothing would be washed first in the hottest water, followed by the darker clothes, with the men's work clothes last. After being washed, the clothes would be put into washtubs with rinse water. Those would be agitated by hand and again wrung out, and then the process was repeated in the second rinse tub. Finally the wet clothing was ready for the wash lines.

Laundry was hung outdoors whenever the weather allowed. Usually there were definite "rules" as to how items should be hung—dark clothing in the shade, whites in the sun, socks together, etc. Women vied with each other for the whitest whites. When the weather was inclement, the clothing was hung in the basement or on lines strung throughout the house. In cold climates, the clothes drying inside provided much needed humidity in the homes. On nice days in winter, clothes were often hung outdoors, even if they froze stiff! It was quite a sight to see a man's pair of overalls standing by themselves when you brought them in from the cold.

How many of you hang clothes outdoors? It's the "green" thing to do, as your dryer takes a great deal of energy to run. I really enjoy hanging wash on the line, and the laundry smells like fresh air and sunshine.
Tip: In cold weather, your quilting gloves keep your hands warm while hanging the laundry outdoors.

My wash lines are famous! You can see them pictured in my *Granny Quilt Decor* book, and they were also featured in an article *American Patchwork & Quilting* magazine wrote when they came to visit me several years ago.

Next time you do laundry, thank your lucky stars you have a truly automatic washing machine!

assembling the quilt, continued

9. Arrange the blocks on point (on the diagonal) with the print triangles along the edge. Use the smaller triangles at the corners. Sew the blocks and triangles together in diagonal rows, alternating the pressing direction of the rows.

10. Trim the edges of the quilt if necessary to straighten, being careful to leave at least a ¼" seam allowance on the outer edge. Measure the width of the quilt through the middle and trim 2 blue solid borders to this measurement. Sew to the top and bottom of the quilt. Press toward the borders.

11. Measure the length of the quilt through the middle. Piece and then trim 2 blue solid borders to this measurement. Sew to the sides of the quilt. Press toward the borders.

12. Add the print borders in the same manner. Press toward the borders.

finishing the quilt

1. Layer, baste and quilt as desired. Baste a scant ¼" from the edge to keep it from stretching.

2. Join the binding strips with diagonal seams pressed open. Press in half for a double binding. Sew to the quilt with a ¼" seam, mitering the corners. See pages 119-121 for instructions on mitering corners and joining binding ends.

3. Trim the excess batting and backing and fold the binding over the raw edges. Stitch down by hand with matching thread.

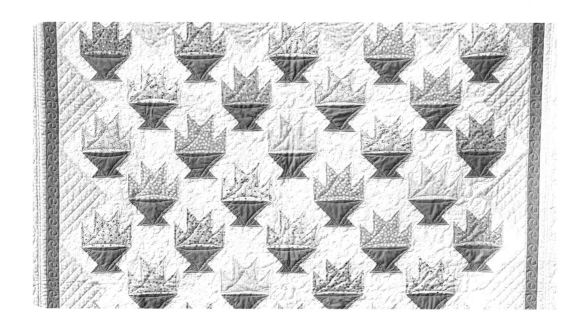

Ironing Day

Don't you wonder who decided that clothing looked better when it was pressed? And why?

A tradition of ironing clothing was well established at least a thousand years ago.

The Chinese used pans filled with hot coals to "iron" stretched cloth (no ironing board). In Europe women used stones, glass or wood for smoothing the wrinkles out of cloth, although they were not heated. It is believed that the flat smoothing stones would be rubbed over fabric to smooth it, polish it or press in pleats, much like we use our small wooden "irons" today. In the eighteenth and nineteenth centuries in Europe, glass smoothers had handles and looked somewhat like darning eggs.

Blacksmiths began making simple flat irons in the late Middle Ages. These flat irons were also known as "sad irons." They would be heated on a stove, used until they cooled and then exchanged for another. In the 1870s Mrs. Potts invented the removable handle for the sad iron, so the handle could be quickly switched to another heated iron base. Using sad irons required you to stand close to a stove where the irons were heated. Not the most comfortable place to be on a hot day!

Not only did the irons need to be heated and then exchanged, but they also needed to be kept clean, sandpapered and polished and regularly lightly greased to avoid rusting. No temperature guides were on the irons, so only experience could tell you when the iron was hot enough to do the job, or when it was too hot and would scorch the fabric. A time-tested method was to spit on the hot metal or hold it up to your hand (but not touch it).

Because sad irons cooled so quickly, "box" or charcoal irons were invented, whereby the iron was heated with charcoal. However, it was a challenge to keep the irons clean enough. It was every woman's dream to have a self-heating iron. Finally, in 1882, an electric iron was invented. By 1892, General Electric was selling an electric iron, but it wasn't until the early 1950s that steam irons became available.

If you are lucky enough to find an old iron in working condition, you'll notice how heavy it is compared to our new irons. They also get hotter and work very nicely for ironing damp cotton fabrics and appliqué (if they don't have the steam holes).

We can be thankful that so many of our garments today are permanent-press or a knit fabric, and rarely do we need to iron our clothing. Our mothers and grandmothers not only had lots of cotton clothing to iron, but also the challenge to iron the gathered skirts, puffy sleeves, fussy collars and other intricate details in the clothing. No surprise that my mother taught all her girls (six of us) to iron our own clothing at a relatively young age.

Before steam irons, all the cotton garments had to be damp to be ironed effectively. My mother used a plastic sprinkling topper on a glass soda bottle, shaking small drops of water over the dried, wrinkled clothing and then wrapping it all in a bag for several hours so all the clothing would be slightly dampened. The hot iron would dry the fabric quickly and take out the wrinkles.

Next time you do laundry, be thankful you don't need to set aside a full day to complete the task of ironing all those clothes. If you are looking for a bit more adventure when ironing, check out the Wii game by Wacky World of Sports—Extreme Ironing. You can pretend you're ironing outdoors in the most unlikely locations!

MILADY'S
fans

Fans are one-fourth of a Dresden Plate. They are easy to make, especially with my quick method of sewing and turning the points for a no-appliqué finish! Fan blocks are interesting, as they are asymmetrical and can be arranged in numerous ways, much like Log-Cabin blocks. Arrange your blocks any way you like and make the quilt in any size—three sizes are given in the pattern.

Tip: Before beginning, choose the size of the quilt you want to make. Go through the pattern and highlight or circle the appropriate numbers (wall/baby, twin, full/queen) to make the cutting and sewing directions easier to follow.

cutting directions

from	cut	yield
background print	(7, 16, 31) 8½"×42" strips	(25, 63, 121)—8½" squares
each fat quarter	two 6"×21" strips	(125, 315, 605) wedges cut with Easy Dresden* (or approximately 18 wedges from each fabric)
lavender solid	(2, 4, 8) 2¼"×42" strips	(25, 63, 121) 2¼" squares

If not using the Easy Dresden tool, use template on page 96.

materials

fabric requirements

BACKGROUND PRINTS
baby/wall: 2¼ yds.
twin: 4½ yds.
full/queen: 8¼ yds.

VARIETY OF PRINTS (FAT QUARTERS)
baby/wall: 7
twin: 18
full/queen: 34

LAVENDER SOLID (FAN BASE, INNER BORDER, BINDING)
baby/wall: 1 yd.
twin: 1⅓ yds.
full/queen: 1¾ yds.

suggested tools
Easy Dresden (EZ Quilting #8829306)
Bamboo Pointer/Creaser (EZ Quilting # 882108)

additional requirements
FUSIBLE WEB OR FREEZER PAPER
baby/wall: ¼ yd.
twin: ½ yd.
full/queen: 1 yd.

finished dimensions
baby/wall: 54" square
twin: 66½"×82½"
full/queen: 98½" square

assembling
the fans

1. Fold the wide edge of each fan right sides together and sew a ¼" seam across the top edge. *(Tip: To eliminate backstitching at the fold, set the stitch length smaller.) (figure 1)*

2. Trim off the folded corner of the wedge and turn the point right-side out (using the Bamboo Pointer/Creaser or similar tool). Center the seam and press. *(figure 1)*

3. Sew 5 of the wedges together to make a fan. Begin stitching ½" below the folded edges, backstitch to the top and then stitch the remainder of the seam. This hides your thread ends. Press the seams all one direction. *(figure 2)*

4. Place the fan in one corner of the background square. Align the edges of the fan with the edges of the square. Baste in place by hand or machine (long stitches). *(figure 3)*

5. Using freezer paper or fusible web, cut (25, 63, 121) 2" squares. Trace (25, 63, 121) quarter circles from the template given on page 96, using a corner of each of the squares aligned with the corner on the quarter circle. Cut out the fusible-web or freezer-paper shapes. *(Tip: You can reuse the freezer-paper templates several times.)*

6. Using a warm iron, press the freezer-paper or fusible-web shapes to the wrong side of the fabric squares, matching up the corners *(figure 4)*. Cut out the exact shape if using fusible web; add a ¼" seam allowance to the curved edge of the freezer-paper templates. If using freezer-paper templates, wet the curved edge of the fabric with a bit of spray starch or diluted liquid starch (1:1) and iron the fabric edge only over the curved edge of the freezer-paper template. Remove the freezer-paper.

7. Fuse or appliqué the fan base in place on the corner of the block. *(figure 5)*

figure 1

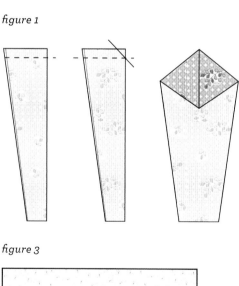

figure 2

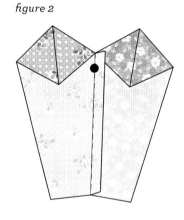

figure 3

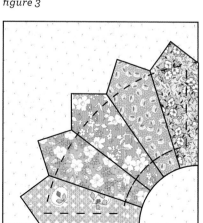

figure 4

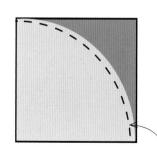

If using freezer paper, add a ¼" seam allowance to curved edge.

assembling the quilt

1. Arrange the fan blocks in any arrangement or as shown in the photo on page 92. The blocks are set 5"×5" for the wall/baby quilt, 7"×9" for the twin size quilt, and 11"×11" for the full/queen size.

2. Sew the blocks together in rows, pressing the seams away from the fans.

3. Sew the rows together and press the seams all one direction.

adding the borders

1. Cut (4, 7, 10) 1½"×42" lavender-solid inner borders. Join the borders with diagonal seams as needed. Measure and trim 2 borders the width of the quilt. Sew to the top and bottom of the quilt. Press toward the borders. Repeat for the sides of the quilt.

2. From each of the fat quarters, cut one 4½"×21" strip. Using the Easy Dresden tool and placing the 6" line at the top (or bottom) of the strip, cut wedges from each fabric.

3. From the background fabric, cut (3, 5, 6) 4½"×42" strips. Using the Easy Dresden tool, and placing the 5" line at the top (or bottom) of the strip, cut those strips into (60, 90, 100) wedges.

4. Beginning and ending with a background wedge and alternating with a print wedge, sew the wedges together, alternating the wide and narrow ends of the wedges. Press the seams toward the print wedges. At the ends of each pieced border, trim the background wedges straight. *(Tip: You can take in or let out seams to adjust the border length slightly.)*

5. Sew the pieced borders to the top and bottom of the quilt. Press the seams toward the inner borders. From the lavender solid, cut one 4½"×42" strip. Cut four 4½" squares. Sew the squares to the ends of the side borders. Press toward the lavender squares.

6. Sew the side borders to the quilt, pressing the seams toward the inner borders.

figure 5

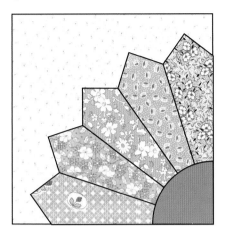

Easy Dresden tool

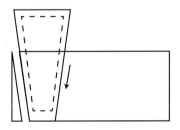

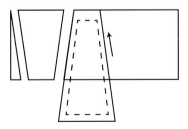

To use the Easy Dresden tool, cut a strip the desired width. For the first cut, align the narrow end of the tool with the bottom of the strip. Cut on both sides of the tool. Rotate the tool so the narrow end is at the top of the strip. Cut again.

finishing
the quilt

1. Piece and trim a backing at least 4" larger than the quilt top. Also trim the batting to the size of the backing.

2. Layer, baste and quilt as desired. On the quilt shown, stitching in the ditch was done between the blocks and between all the wedges, and a line of quilting was stitched along the top edge of the fans. A feather design was quilted in the open area above each fan.

3. Remove the basting stitches.

4. From the lavender solid, cut (6, 8, 10) 2¼"×42" strips for binding. Join with diagonal seams pressed open. Fold the binding in half, wrong sides together, and press.

5. Before binding, hand baste a scant ¼" from the edge of the quilt. Sew the binding to the quilt with a ¼" seam, mitering the corners. Join the binding ends with the "Perfect Fit" technique (see page 120). Sign and date!

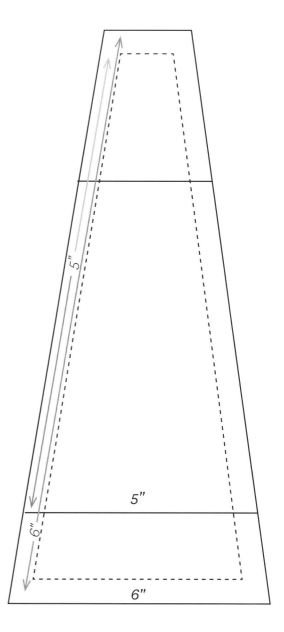

Easy Dresden template

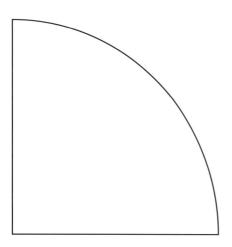

Quarter circle template to use for the base of the fan

variation:
milady's fans
(34" square)

For a new twist on a traditional pattern, choose a group of fabrics that is fun, funky and bright! These bright fabrics turn an old-fashioned pattern into a modern work of art.

cutting directions

from	cut	yield
background	three 8½"×42" strips	nine 8½" squares
each pink print	one 6"×21" strip	nine wedges cut with Easy Dresden*
green print	one 2¼"×42" strip	nine 2¼" squares for fan bases
	four 1¼"×42" strips	inner border
	four 2¼"×42" strips	binding
border stripe	four 4¼"×42" strips	outer border

materials

fabric requirements

background: ¾ yd.

5 pink prints: fat eighths (9"×21")

green print: ⅝ yd.

border stripe: ⅝ yd.

backing: 1 yd.

batting: 35" square

If not using the Easy Dresden tool, use template on page 96.

BLUE-RIBBON
winner

I named this project a Blue-Ribbon Winner because the cheerful ginghams and fruit motifs reminded me of the jams and jellies displayed at a county fair. The printed border makes an easy finish for this tablecloth. The tablecloth is backed (no batting), and a bit of quilting holds the layers together. It could also be finished as a quilt.

cutting directions

from	cut	yield
each background	seven 2"×42" strips	60—2" squares
		60 Companion Angle* triangles
each star print	one 3½"×21" strip	three 3½" squares
	two 2"×21" strips	24 Easy Angle** triangles
each gingham (including dark blue)	five 1½"×42" strips	ten 1½"×6½" rectangles
		ten 1½"×8½" rectangles
dark blue gingham	two 1"×42" strips	four 1"×7" rectangles
		four 1"×6½" rectangles
	seven 2¼"×42" strips	binding
border print	four 7"×46" strips cut lengthwise along selvage	borders
from remainder of border print	two 6½"×28" strips	twelve Flip n Set*** triangles
	one 8½"×28" strip	two 8½" squares, cut once on the diagonal for corner triangles

*If not using the Companion Angle tool, cut 4¼" square. Cut twice on the diagonal like an X.
**If not using the Easy Angle tool, cut 2⅜" squares. Cut once on the diagonal.
***If not using the Flip n Set tool, cut three 13" squares. Cut twice on the diagonal like an X.

materials

fabric requirements

2 backgrounds:
½ yd. each
10 star prints: fat eighths
4 ginghams: ¼ yd. each
dark blue gingham: ⅞ yd.
border print: 2⅔ yds.
backing: 3⅔ yds.
batting: twin size

suggested tools

Easy Angle (EZ Quilting #8823759)
Companion Angle (EZ Quilting #882670139)
Flip n Set (EZ Quilting #8823755)

finished dimensions

58" square (8½" blocks)

assembling the blocks

1. Sew the star-print triangles on both sides of the larger background triangles. Press. *(figure 1)*

2. Sew two Step 1 units to opposite sides of the matching 3½" print squares. Press. *(figure 2)*

3. Sew background squares to the remainder of the star-point units. Press. *(figure 3)*

4. Sew the Step 2 and 3 units to make star blocks. Make 30. At this point the blocks should measure 6½" square. *(figure 4)*

5. Sew 1½"×6½" gingham rectangles to opposite sides of each of 25 blocks. Press. *(figure 5)*

6. Sew the 1½"×8½" matching gingham rectangles to the remaining 2 sides of the blocks. Press. They should measure 8½" square. *(figure 6)*

figure 1

figure 2

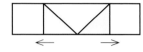
figure 3

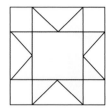
figure 4

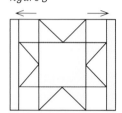
figure 5

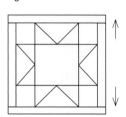
figure 6

assembling the quilt

1. Arrange the star blocks and large triangles in diagonal rows. (Save 5 blocks for the border.) *(Tip: Alternate the long and short sides of the blocks.)* Sew the blocks together in rows, alternating the direction the seams are pressed. Sew the rows together. Press all one direction. Add the corner triangles last. Press.

2. Trim the edges straight, leaving at least a ¼" seam allowance from the corners of the blocks.

3. Measure and trim all 4 borders to the width of the quilt. Sew 2 borders to opposite sides of the quilt. Press toward the borders.

4. Sew blue gingham 1" wide rectangles to adjacent sides of the last 4 blocks (you will have one block left over). Press. Sew to the ends of the remaining 2 borders, with the blue gingham toward the inside of the quilt. Press toward the borders. Sew the borders to the quilt, pressing the seams toward the borders.

finishing the quilt

1. Layer, baste and quilt as desired. Join the binding ends with diagonal seams pressed open. Press the binding in half, wrong sides together. Sew to the quilt with a ¼" seam, mitering the corners. See pages 119-121 for more instructions on mitering corners and joining binding ends.

2. Trim the excess batting and backing, turn the binding to the back side and stitch down by hand with matching thread.

variation:
blue-ribbon winner
(48"×59")

For a completely different look from the original quilt, I used soft romantic pastels.

cutting directions

from	cut	yield
white	nine 2"×42" strips	72—2" squares
	two 6½"×42" strips	72 Companion Angle* triangles
	three 8½"×42" strips	ten Flip n Set** triangles
		two 8½" squares cut once on the diagonal
pink, yellow and blue florals	one 3½"×42" strip each	six 3½" squares
	two 2"×42" strips	48 Easy Angle*** triangles
blue, tiny floral	15—1½"×42" strips	36—1½"×8½" rectangles
		36—1½"×6½" rectangles
pink, tiny floral	five 1¼"×42" strips	inner border
	1¼" bias strips	250" of binding
blue floral	four 7"×60" strips cut lengthwise	outer border

materials

fabric requirements

white print (stars, setting triangles): 1¼ yds.

yellow and pink floral (stars):
¼ yd. each

blue floral (stars, wide border): 2 yds.

blue tiny floral (star frames): ¾ yd.

pink tiny floral (inner border, binding): ¾ yd.

backing: 3 yds.

*If not using the Companion Angle tool, cut 4 ¼" squares. Cut twice on the diagonal like an X.
** If not using the Flip n Set tool, cut three 13" squares. Cut twice on the diagonal like an X.
***If not using the Easy Angle tool, cut 2⅜" squares. Cut once on the diagonal.

TIPTOE THROUGH
the flowers

Create your own flower garden right in your sewing room! Using a variety of fabrics, make each "flower" different. The flower blocks are easy to make—and if you choose—you can make this quilt bed-sized. Notice the small flowers in the pieced border—if you shy away from pieced borders because you're afraid they won't fit, try my secret tip on making any pieced border fit the quilt.

Tip: Before beginning, choose the size of the quilt you want to make. Go through the pattern and highlight or circle the appropriate numbers corresponding (lap, twin/full, queen) to the size you are making. This will make the cutting and sewing directions easier to follow.

cutting directions for blocks

from	cut	yield
each (30, 60, 90) print	two 2½"×21" strips	two 2½"×6½" rectangles
		two 2½"×4½" rectangles
		three 2½" squares
yellow solid (3, 4, 5)	(2, 4, 6) 2½"×42" strips	(30, 60, 90) 2½" squares
background	(15, 30, 45) 2"×42 strips	(240, 480, 720) Companion Angle* triangles
	(5, 9, 13) 2¼"×42" strips	(120, 240, 360) Easy Angle** triangles
	(13, 25, 41) 2"×42" strips	(49, 97, 161) 2"×9" sashes
	(6, 8, 10) 3"×42" strips	inner border

*If not using the Companion Angle tool, cut 4¼" square. Cut twice on the diagonal like an X.
**If not using the Easy Angle tool, cut 2⅝" squares. Cut once on the diagonal.

Cutting chart continued on page 104»

materials

fabric requirements

prints: (30, 60, 90) fat eighths

YELLOW SOLID
lap: 1⅛ yds.
twin/full: 1⅓ yds.
queen: 1¾ yds.

BACKGROUND
lap: 3⅓ yds.
twin/full: 5⅔ yds.
queen: 8¼ yds.

BACKING
lap: 3¾ yds.
twin/full: 7⅓ yds.
queen: 9¼ yds.

BATTING
twin/full
queen
king

suggested tools
Easy Angle (EZ Quilting #8823759)

Companion Angle (EZ Quilting #882670139)

finished dimensions
8½" finished block

lap quilt: 62½"×74"
(set 5 blocks ×6 blocks)

twin/full quilt: 83"×94½"
(set 7 blocks ×8 blocks)

queen quilt: 103"×114½"
(set 9 blocks ×10 blocks)

piecing the blocks

1. Sew a yellow square between two matching print 2½"×6½" rectangles. Press toward the yellow square. Repeat for (30, 60, 90) units. *(figure 1)*

2. Sew Companion Angle triangles to both ends of the print rectangles and 2 of the 2½" squares as shown. Press toward the print rectangles and squares. *(figures 2 and 3)*

3. Join Step 1 and 2 units of the same print, matching the centers. Press toward the center of the block. *(figure 4)*

4. Center and sew smaller Easy Angle triangles to the corners. Press toward the corner triangles. Make (30, 60, 90) blocks. Trim each block to 9" square (or all the same size), allowing a ¼" seam allowance on the outside edge of the block. *(figure 5)*

5. Trim the remaining (30, 60, 90) 2½" print squares to 2" for cornerstones. Sew sashing strips between (5, 7, 9) blocks for the horizontal rows. Make (6, 8, 10) horizontal rows. Press toward the sashing. *(figure 6)*

6. Sew (5, 7, 9) sashing strips together with cornerstones between. Press toward the sashing. Make (5, 7, 9) horizontal sashing rows. *(figure 7)*

7. Sew the block rows and sashing rows together, pinning and matching seams. Press the seams toward the sashing strips. (You will have four blocks left over in the twin/full size.)

8. Piece, measure, trim and sew the inner border strips to the quilt.

cutting directions for flower border

from	cut	yield
each print	one 2½"×21" strip	eight 2½" squares
yellow solid	(3, 4, 5) 2½"×42" strips	(40, 54, 72) 2½" squares
	one 6¼"×42" strip	four 6¼" squares for corners
	(7, 9, 11) 2¼"×42" strips	binding
background	(3, 4, 5) 2½"×42" strips	(36, 50, 68) 2½" squares
	(10, 14, 18) 2"×42" strips	(160, 216, 288) Companion Angle** triangles
	(1,1,1) 2¼"×42" strip	(16) Easy Angle* triangles

*If not using the Easy Angle tool, cut 2 ⅝" squares. Cut once on the diagonal.
**If not using the Companion Angle tool, cut 4¼" square. Cut twice on the diagonal like an X.

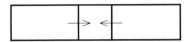

figure 1

figure 2

figure 3

figure 4

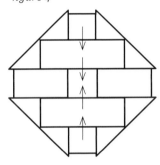

figure 5

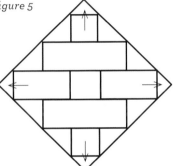

figure 6

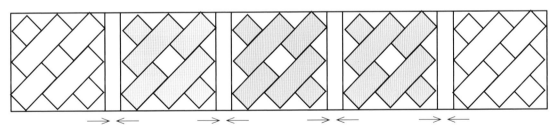

figure 7

assembling the
flower border

1. Sew matching print squares on opposite sides of a yellow square. Sew Companion Angle triangles to each end as shown. Press toward the print squares. *(figure 8)*

2. Sew 2 different prints on opposite sides of a background square. Sew Companion Angle triangles to each end as shown. Press toward the print squares. *(figure 9)*

3. Sew the Step 1 and 2 units together as shown, pinning and matching seams. *(figure 10)* Sew (9, 13, 16) flowers together for the top and bottom rows, starting and ending each row as shown. Press the seams all one direction. *(figure 11)* Sew (11, 14, 18) flowers together for the side borders.

4. Trim all 4 edges of the border strips evenly, allowing a ¼" seam around all 4 sides. Measure the top and bottom flower borders. Trim the quilt top the same amount on each long side to equal the measurement of the top and bottom borders. Repeat with the side borders. *(Note: You are adjusting the size of the quilt to fit the borders, not making the borders fit the quilt.)*

5. Sew the top and bottom flower borders to the quilt. Press toward the inner border. Sew the yellow 6¼" squares to the ends of the side flower borders. Press toward the squares. Sew the side flower borders to the quilt. Press toward the inner border. *(figure 11)*

figure 8

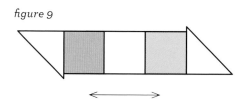

figure 9

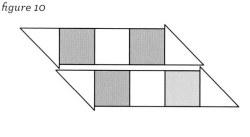

figure 10

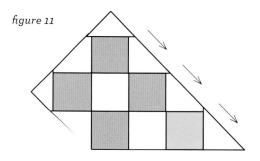

figure 11

finishing
the quilt

1. Layer, baste and quilt as desired. After quilting, baste a scant ¼" from the edge of the quilt to hold the layers together. Mark a diagonal line on each corner. Trim away the corners ¼" outside the marked line.

2. Join the binding ends with diagonal seams pressed open. Press in half for double binding. Sew to the quilt with a ¼" seam allowance, mitering the corners. See pages 118-119 for more instructions on making binding and mitering corners. End the binding with the "Perfect Fit" technique on pages 120-121.

3. Trim the excess batting and backing, turn the binding to the back side and stitch down by hand with matching thread.

Garden Sunshine
....

Now, I'll be the first to admit I don't have a green thumb. I can't keep houseplants alive (unless they're the plastic variety), and I don't have any success with growing vegetables. But I do have a flower garden, because what is life without flowers? Below is a gardening tip everyone can use.

The Garden of Daily Living
(author unknown)

Plant Three Rows of Peas
    1. Peas of mind
    2. Peas of heart
    3. Peas of soul

Plant Four Rows of Squash
    1. Squash gossip
    2. Squash indifference
    3. Squash grumbling
    4. Squash selfishness

Plant Four Rows of Lettuce
    1. Lettuce be faithful
    2. Lettuce be kind
    3. Lettuce be patient
    4. Lettuce really love one another

Plant Three Rows of Turnips
    1. Turnip for meetings
    2. Turnip for service
    3. Turnip to help one another

Plant Four Rows of Thyme
    1. Thyme for each other
    2. Thyme for family
    3. Thyme for friends
    4. Thyme for God

Water freely with patience and cultivate with love because you reap what you sow.

picnic
QUILT

If you're looking for an easy quilt, this is it! No triangles, no tricky piecing, but instead an easy pattern that really showcases the fabric! It is quick to put together to use on a bed, as a throw or as a picnic quilt.

cutting directions

from	cut	yield
red solid	twelve 1½"×42" strips	93—1½"×4½" sashes
	20—1½"×42" strips	vertical sashes
	seven 2½"×42" strips	outer border
	seven 2¼"×42" strips	binding
each fat quarter	two 6½"×21" strips	eight 4½"×6½" rectangles
		one 3"×4½" rectangle

materials

fabric requirements

assorted prints: 12 fat quarters
red solid: 2½ yds.
backing: 3½ yds.
twin-size batting

finished dimensions

66"×58"

assembling the rows

1. Sew together nine assorted print 4½"×6½" rectangles and eight 1½"×4½" red solid sashes to make a long vertical row. Press the seams toward the red sashes. Make a total of 6 rows. *(figure 1)*

2. Sew together 8 assorted print rectangles, 9 1½"×4½" red solid sashes, and two 3"×4½" print rectangles at the ends to make a long vertical row. Press the seams toward the sashes. Make a total of 5 rows. *(figure 2)*

3. Join the remaining 1½"×42" red strips with diagonal seams pressed open. Trim ten strips to the length of the vertical rows 62½" (or take an average of the lengths, if they differ). Sew the vertical sashes between the rows, starting and ending with a Step 1 row and alternating with the Step 2 rows. (Refer to the quilt photo on page 108.) Press toward the sashing rows. (*Tip: Sew the long vertical seams with the print rectangles on top to prevent stretching the sashing.*)

adding the borders

1. Join the 2½" wide red solid border strips with diagonal seams pressed open. Measure the quilt width through the center of the quilt. Trim 2 borders to this measurement. Sew to the top and bottom of the quilt. Press the seams toward the red solid borders.

2. Measure the quilt length through the center of the quilt. Trim two 2½" wide red solid borders to this length. Sew to the sides of the quilt. Press the seams toward the red solid borders.

finishing the quilt

1. Cut the backing piece into two 1¾ yd. pieces. Trim off the selvage on one side of each piece. Join those two pieces on the trimmed edge with a ½" seam. Press the seam open.

2. Layer the backing (wrong-side up), the batting and the quilt top (right-side up). Baste.

3. Quilt as desired. (The quilt shown was machine quilted in an all-over pattern with dark tan thread.)

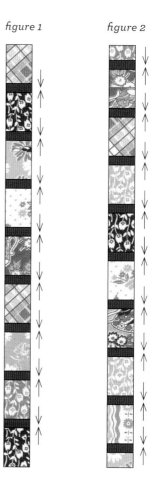

figure 1   *figure 2*

binding

1. Before binding, hand baste a scant ¼" from the edge of the quilt to hold the layers together.

2. Join the 2¼" wide red binding strips with diagonal seams pressed open. Press in half, wrong sides together, to make a double bias binding.

3. Sew the binding to the quilt with a generous ¼" seam, mitering the corners. See page 119 for more instructions.

4. For more instructions on joining binding ends with the "Perfect Fit" technique, see pages 120.

5. Trim excess batting and backing and turn to the back side. Stitch down by hand with machine thread.

recipe

pulled pork sandwiches

4 lbs. boneless pork roast

1 tsp. salt

1 tbsp. paprika

1 tsp. pepper

¼ cup brown sugar

1 tbsp. dry mustard powder

Put the dry ingredients in a slow cooker, mix, then rub all over the pork roast.

In medium bowl, whisk together:

1 tsp. salt

1 cup cider vinegar

1 tsp. pepper

½ cup ketchup

1 tbsp. brown sugar

Pour into slow-cooker with roast and add ¾ cup water. Cover and cook on low for 8-10 hours. Remove any fat and shred the meat with two forks. Serve hot in buns.

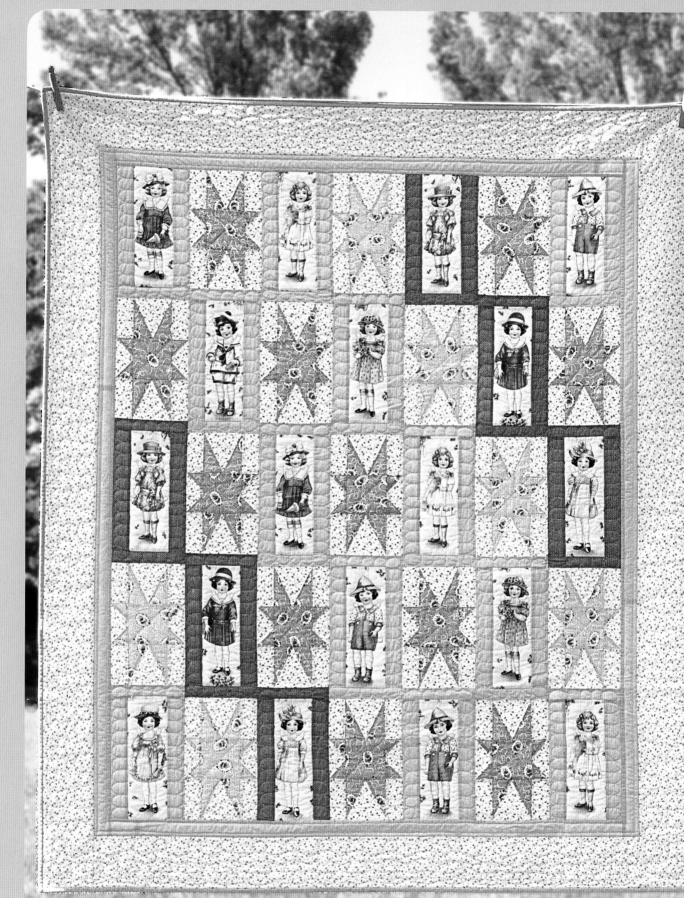

DANCING WITH
the stars

This sweet quilt incorporates adorable paper doll blocks alternated with stretched star blocks. The children are all framed to make them the same size as the star blocks, and then the rows are set together vertically. You could incorporate any themed fabric in place of the paper doll, as long as the block with the frame is the same size as the star blocks.

cutting directions

from	cut	yield
paper doll print	fussy-cut	18 dolls (4"×11" rectangles)
each diagonal plaid	one 11"×42" strip	twelve 2"×11" rectangles
		ten 1½"×7" rectangles
plaid 3	six 2"×42" strips	inner border
	seven 2¼"×42" strips	binding
each background print	three 4"×42" strips	twelve Tri* triangles
		36—2"×4" rectangles
background print 3	six 5"×42" strips	outer border
each star print	two 4"×42" strips	six 4" squares
		twelve pairs Recs* triangles
	two 2"×21" strips	24—2" squares

If not using the Tri-Recs tool, use the templates on page 114.

materials

fabric requirements

background prints 1-2: ⅜ yd.

background print 3: 1⅓ yds.

3 star prints: ⅜ yd.

diagonal plaids 1-2: ⅜ yd.

diagonal plaid 3: 1¼ yds.

paper doll (theme) fabric: 1¼ yds.

backing: 3½ yds.

batting: twin-size

suggested tools

Tri-Recs (EZ Quilting #8823753)

finished dimensions

57½"×68½"

assembling the paper doll blocks

1. Sew matching 2"×11" diagonal plaid strips to both sides of the "paper doll" rectangles. Press toward the sashing. Make 18. *(figure 1)*

assembling the star blocks

1. Choose a background fabric to coordinate with each star print. Assemble all the Tri-Recs units. They should measure 4" square at this point. *(figure 2)*

2. Using the same combination of fabrics as in Step 1, sew a 2" star print square on opposite ends of one of the 2"×4" background rectangles as shown. Sew on the diagonal. Trim the excess seam allowance and press toward the green triangles. Make 36. *(figure 3)*

3. Assemble and press the star blocks as shown. At this point they should measure 7"×11". Make 18. *(figure 4)*

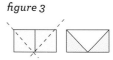

figure 1   *figure 2*

figure 3

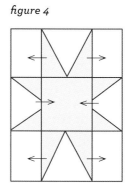

figure 4

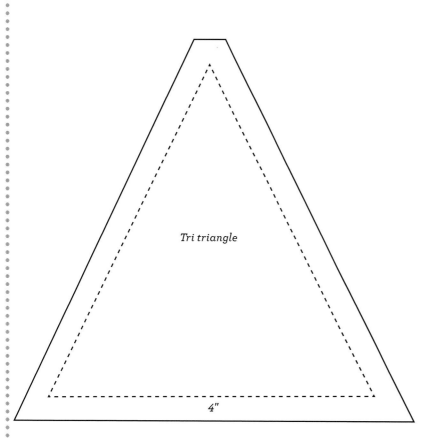

Tri triangle

4"

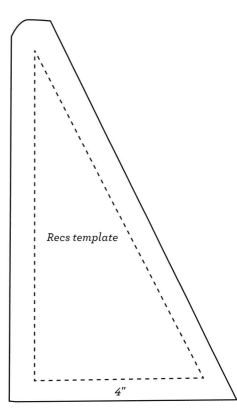

Recs template

4"

assembling the quilt

1. Arrange the paper doll blocks and star blocks in 7 *vertical* rows as shown in the quilt photo (page 112). You will have 1 star block left over. Sew horizontal diagonal plaid sashes on one or both ends of the paper doll blocks, but not when the paper doll blocks are at the top or bottom edges. Press toward the paper doll block.

2. Sew the blocks in each *vertical* row together. Press the seams toward the sashing. Sew the rows together, pinning and matching seam allowances.

3. Piece, measure and trim two #3 plaid borders the width of the quilt. Sew to the top and bottom of the quilt. Press toward the borders. Add side borders and the wider outer borders in the same manner.

finishing the quilt

1. Layer, baste and quilt as desired.

2. Join the binding strips with diagonal seams pressed open. Sew to the quilt with a ¼" seam allowance, mitering the corners. (See pages 119-121 for more instructions on mitering and joining binding ends.)

3. Trim the excess batting and backing, turn the binding over the back side and stitch down with matching thread.

Paper Dolls

The paper-doll fabric was inspired by a vintage book of paper dolls I found. Their beautifully designed clothing and charming faces appeal to everyone, especially if you remember playing with paper dolls as a child. This set of paper dolls was printed during the peak of their popularity, "The Golden Age of Paper Dolls," between 1930 and 1950. During the Great Depression and WWII when money was tight, paper dolls were inexpensive toys that provided many happy hours of fun.

Paper dolls can be traced back to 900 BC in Japan when a purification ceremony used a paper figure and a kimono like object in a boat.

In the 1700s, paper dolls appeared in France as hand-painted figures and costumes created for the entertainment of adults or to show current fashions. In 1791 there emerged the English Fashion Doll, an 8" female figure printed on cardboard and jointed with thread. The dolls came with a complete wardrobe and would sell for about fifteen dollars in today's money.

In London in 1810, the S. & J. Fuller & Company printed the first commercial paper doll in book form. Along with the wardrobe was a moral tale of "Little Fanny"; the book sold for thirteen to twenty-two dollars.

In the United States, the McLoughlin Bros. started printing paper dolls, selling them at five to ten cents a set, making them very popular and affordable for all children. Some were printed in beautiful color, others in black and white, and were hand tinted. Civil War widows often earned money by painting or coloring the printed paper dolls.

It is interesting to note that early paper-doll clothing did not have tabs to hold the garments on the dolls. Instead children painstakingly attached the clothes with tiny drops of sealing wax.

In the 1830s a doll was printed portraying a famous ballerina. Since then, celebrity dolls continue to be made, including the present day.

In 1859, *Godey's Lady's Book* was the first known magazine to print a paper doll and clothing. This set the trend for many magazines in the 1900s to print paper dolls, along with a story about the dolls and their extended families—some stories continued in serial form. *Woman's Home Companion* carried the famous "Kewpie" dolls in the early 1900s.

Perhaps you remember the Betsy McCall doll in *McCall's* magazine? She debuted in 1951 and continued through the late 1990s. Children's magazines, such as *Jack and Jill*, also printed paper dolls, as did a few newspapers. Paper dolls were even used to advertise products such Baker's chocolate, Pillsbury flour and Singer sewing machines.

Sadly the popularity of paper dolls waned in the 1960s when Barbie dolls were introduced, although paper dolls are still found on toy shelves and in bookstores today.

general instructions

Choosing Fabric
Publishing a book is a long process. If identical fabrics are no longer available, don't despair! Choose similar fabrics if you like the original quilt, or be daring and choose a different colorway for an interesting variation. Whatever fabrics you choose, buy the best quality. Quality fabrics will be easier to sew, and you will have a better finished product. The colors will last longer, and the fabric will hold up well to wear and tear.

Preparing the Fabric
You may choose to prewash your fabric—or not. It is a personal decision. The fabric will lose some body, and you may have some shrinking and unraveling. You can restore the body with a little spray starch or fabric sizing, but don't leave such products in the finished quilt long-term—they may attract dirt and bugs. You can test a fabric for color bleeding by spritzing a small area with water and then ironing it, right sides together, with a white fabric. If there is color transference, it would be safer to prewash. Ironing the folds out of the fabric is a necessary step for accurate cutting.

Cutting
Accuracy in cutting is important for the pieces to fit together properly in your quilt. Some tips for accurate cutting:

• Work in good light—daylight, if possible.

• Iron the fabrics before cutting.

• Cut only two layers of fabric at a time. Any time saved in cutting more layers will be lost when trying to fit together the inaccurate pieces.

• Keep your tools from slipping. Use a film or sandpaper that adheres to the back of the tools.

• Use a sharp rotary cutter and a good mat. Mats and cutting blades do wear out over time, so replace them as needed.

Using the Tools
For most of the projects in this book, you will need a self-healing mat, rotary cutter, various sizes of quilting rulers, a sewing machine, scissors, pins and other notions. These items are all easily found at your local craft retailers.

Use a rotary cutter only on a self-healing mat to avoid damage to your cutting surface. When cutting, push away from you with the blade—this will help minimize the potential for injury. When cutting a straight edge, slide the rotary cutter blade down the edge of an acrylic quilting ruler, being sure to keep your fingers out of the way.

Any additional tool requirements or suggestions are found in the project sections. A short tutorial on two of these tools is found on page 123.

Sewing
Quarter-inch seams are so important! If at all possible, find a ¼" foot for your machine, made specifically for quilt piecing. They are well worth the small investment. (See tip on opposite page)

If you have problems with the "mad feed dogs" chewing up your fabric, try these tricks to tame them:

• Insert a new needle—a sharps or quilting needle. An 80/12 would be a good size.

• Clean and oil your sewing machine; particularly clean under the throat plate.

• Chain sew whenever possible.

• Begin and end with a scrap of fabric.

Unsewing
It's a fact of life: Mistakes happen. Use a seam ripper when necessary. Strive for perfection and then learn from your mistakes, but also forgive yourself for not being perfect. The Amish place a deliberate mistake in a quilt as a "humility block" because they believe only God is perfect.

Pressing
Remember that the purpose of pressing is to make the seam, unit, block and quilt top as flat as possible. Iron from the right side whenever possible. Follow the pressing arrows given in the directions. If you follow these, most, if not all, of your seams will alternate.

Twisting the Seam

Try this trick whenever you have any type of four-patch unit. It will make the center seam intersection lie flatter.

1. Before pressing the last seam on a four-patch, grasp the seam with both hands about 1" from the center seam. Twist in opposite directions, opening a few threads in the seam. *(figure 1)*

2. Press one seam in one direction and the other seam in the opposite direction. In the center you will see a tiny four-patch appear, and the center now lies very flat. *(figure 2)*

Borders

We often make adding borders to a quilt more difficult than it needs to be. Simply cut the strips designated for the borders and piece them as needed. Some people prefer to piece the borders on the diagonal, but the print can also be matched with a straight seam. Choose which method works best for your project.

Place the border strips on top of the quilt to measure the length or width of the quilt through the middle. Always measure with two border strips together so the borders are guaranteed to be the same length. Crease the border strips at the proper length, but cut an extra inch longer for leeway. Pin the borders to the quilt and sew.

Batting

The type of batting you use is a personal choice. Cotton batting will give you a flat, traditional look and will shrink a bit when you wash the quilt, resulting in a slightly puckered look. Cotton batting is more difficult to hand quilt, but it will machine quilt nicely because the layers of the quilt will not shift.

Polyester batting has a bit more loft (puffiness) than a cotton batting and is easier to hand quilt. However, it is more slippery, which can cause shifting when machine quilting. Combination poly-and-cotton battings can give you the best qualities of both and are a good choice for hand and machine quilting.

Quilting

After you have finished your quilt top, it's time to consider quilting. Some tops need to be marked for quilting before they are basted, others while they are being quilted. Whichever device you use, test it on scraps of fabric from the project to check if it can be easily removed.

Create your "quilt sandwich" by layering the batting between the quilt top and the backing fabric and basting the layers together with safety pins or thread 4" apart. The batting and backing should be cut at least 4" larger than the quilt top.

Some of the quilts in this book were hand quilted, while others were machine quilted on a sewing machine, and still others were sent out to a long-arm quilter. Feel free to create your own quilting designs.

figure 1

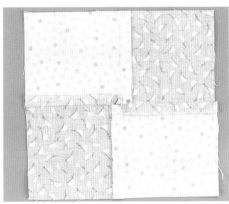

figure 2

Try This!

Try this quick check to see if you are sewing an exact ¼" seam allowance: Cut three 1½" x 3½" strips. Sew them together on the long edges. Press. The square should now measure 3½". If not, adjust your seam allowance. (Also check that you have pressed correctly.)

Binding

Generally I use double bias or double straight-of-grain binding for any straight edges and single bias binding for curved edges.

1. To cut bias binding, trim off the selvages and trim both the bottom and top edges of the fabric chosen for the binding. Using the 45-degree line on your long ruler, align it with the edge of the fabric and cut off the corner at a 45-degree angle. The fabric should be opened, cutting through a single layer. *(figure 1)*

2. Set the corner aside for another use and cut binding strips from the remainder of the fabric *(figure 2a)*, folding the fabric along the cut edge as needed to shorten the cut. *(figure 2b)*

3. After the strips have been cut, join the angled ends exactly as shown *(figure 3a)*. Sew from the V at the top of the strip to the V at the bottom of the strip (the seam allowance does not have to be ¼"). Join all the strips in this manner to make a continuous binding strip. Press the seams open. *(figure 3b)*

4. To make a double binding, fold the binding in half, wrong sides together, and press. *(figure 4)*

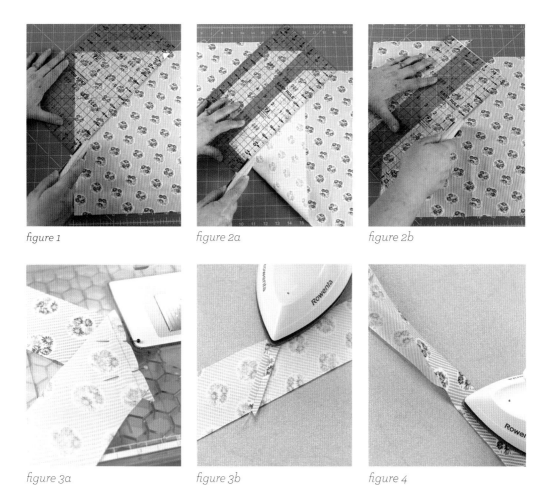

figure 1   figure 2a   figure 2b

figure 3a   figure 3b   figure 4

Mitering Corners on Binding

1. When the quilting is completed, baste a scant ¼" around the perimeter of the quilt to prevent the layers from shifting while the binding is being sewn on. This prevents the edge from stretching. Leave the excess batting and backing in place until after the binding is sewn on so you can trim off the exact amount needed to completely fill the binding. *(figure 1)*

2. Begin sewing the binding to the quilt in the middle of one side, matching the raw edges of the binding to the raw edge of the quilt top. Leave a 6"-8" tail at the beginning. *(figure 2)*

3. To miter a corner, stitch to within a seam's allowance from the corner, stop and backstitch. *(figure 3)*

4. Remove the quilt from under the presser foot and trim the threads. Turn the quilt 90 degrees and pull the binding straight up, forming a 45-degree angle at the corner. *(figure 4)*

5. Fold the binding back down, with the fold on the previously stitched edge of the quilt. Begin stitching at the fold. This will build in enough extra binding to turn the corner. *(figure 5)*

6. For corners that are not square (such as on a table runner), stitch the first edge, stop a seam's allowance from the corner and remove the quilt from under the presser foot. Pull the binding straight up and then fold it back down along the next edge. The fold should now come right to the corner of the quilt. It will not align with the previous edge as in a square corner, but rather at right angles to the next edge. Begin stitching at the previous edge.

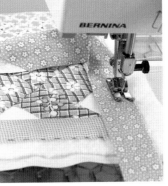

figure 2

figure 3

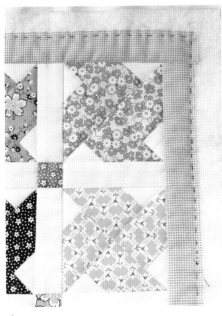

figure 1

figure 4

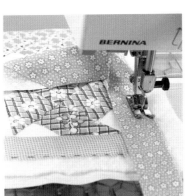

figure 5

"Perfect Fit" Binding

1. When you are within 8"-10" of where you began binding, stop stitching. Remove the quilt from under the presser foot and trim the threads. *(figure 1)*

2. On a flat surface, have the binding ends meet in the center of that unstitched area, leaving a scant ¼" between them. Fold the ends over and crease them where they almost meet. *(figure 2)*

3. Cut one end off at the fold. Then, using the end you have just cut off (open it, if it is a double binding), use it to measure a binding's width away from the fold. Cut off the second end at that measurement. *(figure 3)*

4. Join the ends at right angles with right sides together. Stitch a diagonal seam. *(figure 4)* Check if the seam is sewn correctly before trimming it to a ¼" seam allowance. Finger press the seam open and reposition the binding on the quilt.

5. Finish stitching the binding to the edge of the quilt. *(figure 5)*

6. Trim the excess batting and backing. On the top side of the quilt, press the binding away from the edge of the quilt to make it easier to stitch on the back side. *(figure 6)*

7. On the back side of the quilt, fold the binding over the edge so it covers the stitching line. Hand sew or machine sew the binding in place with matching thread. *(figure 7)*

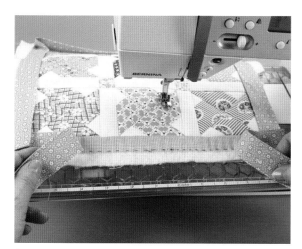

figure 1

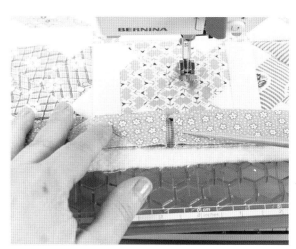

figure 2

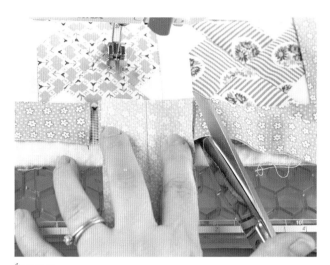

figure 3

figure 4

figure 5

figure 6

figure 7

Try This!

- Use appliqué sharps to hand stitch the binding. These long, thin needles are designed for this type of stitching.

- When stitching the binding down by hand, keep the body of the quilt away from you, holding only the binding edge. You'll find it easier to stitch.

- Use binding clips instead of stick pins to hold the binding edge down for sewing and to avoid poking yourself!

Binding a Scalloped or Curved Edge

1. Do not cut on the marked line! Quilt; then before binding, hand baste along the marked line to keep the layers from shifting when the binding is attached. A bias binding is a must for binding curved edges. Cut a 1¼" single bias binding.

2. With the raw edges of the binding aligned with the marked line on your quilt, begin sewing a ¼" seam. Stitch to the base of the V, and stop with the needle down. Lift the presser foot.

3. Pivot the quilt and binding around the needle. Put the presser foot down and begin stitching out of the V, taking care not to stitch any pleats into the binding. *(figure 1)*

4. Continue around the quilt in this manner, easing the binding around the curves and pivoting at the inside of the V.

5. Trim the seam allowance an even ¼", turn the binding to the back side and stitch down by hand with matching thread, covering the stitching line. At the V, the binding will just fold over upon itself, making a little pleat.

Freezer-Paper Appliqué

1. Trace the shapes on the dull side of the freezer paper, reversing the image first if necessary. (You can reuse the freezer paper several times.) *(Tip: If you iron two pieces of freezer paper together [dull side to shiny side], you'll have a much firmer template to iron the fabric around.)*

2. Cut out the shapes on the marked line. Iron the shapes to the wrong side of the fabrics chosen for the appliqué, leaving at least ¾" between the shapes.

3. Cut out the shapes, adding a scant ¼" seam allowance. Clip any inside curves.

4. With equal parts liquid starch and water mixture (or spray starch) and a cotton swab or child's paintbrush, wet the seam allowance of the appliqué piece. Using the tip of the iron, press the seam allowance over the edge of the freezer paper. Once the edge is well pressed, remove the freezer paper and iron from the right side.

5. Baste in place on the background square either with needle and thread or with basting glue.

6. Appliqué down by hand or machine zigzag with matching or invisible thread.

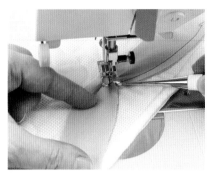

figure 1

Quilt Labels

Your quilts are your legacy—sign them! A label should include the following:

• Names of quilt recipient and quilt maker

• Date of completion/presentation

• Where the quilt was made

• Special occasion or story

You can purchase fabric labels or create your own. Sew or appliqué the label to the quilt either before or after the quilt is completed.

Fusible Appliqué

1. Trace the reversed pattern on the paper side of the fusible web. Leave a bit of space between each appliqué pattern.

2. Cut out the pattern, leaving a small excess of paper around the appliqué. For a softer appliqué, cut out the center of the appliqué shape, leaving at least a ¼" margin inside the shape. Iron to the wrong side of the fabrics chosen for the appliqué, following the manufacturer's instructions for fusing.

3. Cut out the shape on the marked line and then peel off the paper backing. Position the appliqué shape in place on the background fabric and fuse in place, following the manufacturer's directions.

4. By machine or hand, buttonhole stitch around the shapes with contrasting, matching or invisible thread.

Easy Angle tool

Easy Angle allows you to cut triangles from the same size strip as for squares. You need only to add a ½" seam allowance when using Easy Angle, instead of the ⅞" added when not using the tool.

To use the tool most efficiently, layer the fabric strips you are cutting for your triangles right sides together and then cut with Easy Angle. Now they are ready to be chain sewn.

Before making the first cut, trim off the selvages. Then align the top flat edge of the tool at the top of the strip matching a line on the tool with the bottom edge of the strip. Cut on the diagonal edge. *(figure 1)*

To make the second cut, rotate the tool so the flat edge is aligned at the bottom of the strip and a line on the tool is aligned with the top of the strip. Cut again. *(figure 2)*

Continue in this manner down the strip. Chain sew the triangles on the longest edge. Press toward the darkest fabric and trim the dog-ears.

Companion Angle tool

Companion Angle allows you to cut quarter-square triangles with the longest edge on the straight-of-grain. A common use for this type of triangle is the goose in flying geese.

To cut with Companion Angle, align the top flat point of the tool with the top edge of the strip. A line on the tool should align with the bottom of the strip. Cut on both sides of the tool. *(figure 3)*

For the next cut, rotate the tool so the point of the tool is at the bottom of the strip and a line on the tool is aligned with the top of the strip. Cut again. *(figure 4)*

Continue in this manner down the strip of fabric.

figure 3

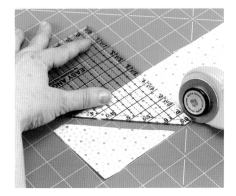

figure 1

figure 4

figure 2

resources

The tools and supplies shown in this book are from the following manufacturers. They can be found at your local quilt shop, fabric or craft store, on the web or by mail order.

American & Efird, Inc.
(A&E Threads)
P.O. Box 507
Mt. Holly, NC 28120
(800) 438-5868
www.amefird.com

Robert Kaufman Fabrics
129 W. 132nd St.
Los Angeles, CA 90061
(800) 877-2066
www.robertkaufman.com

EZ Quilting by Simplicity
6050 Dana Way
Antioch, TN 37013
(800) 628-9362
www.simplicity.com

United Notions
13800 Hutton Dr.
Dallas, TX 75234
(800) 527-9447
www.unitednotions.com

Fairfield Processing Corp.
P.O. Box 1157
88 Rose Hill Ave.
Danbury, CT 06813
(800) 980-8000
www.fairfieldworld.com

Needlings, Inc.
P.O. Box 99
Fairfax, MN 55332
www.feedsacklady.com

Michael Miller Fabrics LLC.
118 W. 22nd St., 5th Floor
New York, NY 10011
(212) 704-0774
www.michaelmillerfabrics.com

index

acknowledgments

My thanks go to all my quilting friends who have asked for another book. A big thank you goes to the following people who have been so instrumental in making the book happen. Thank you!

My editor, Julie Hollyday, and everyone else at F+W Media who worked their magic on my humble projects.

Robert Kaufman Fabric Co. marketing and fabric departments for all their time, talents and assistance with the Clothesline Club over the years.

Rachel Shelburne and Heidi Pridemore (The Whimsical Workshop) for sharing their precise illustrations and Word files.

Bernina USA for the loan of a sewing machine.

Fairfield Corp. for providing batting for the projects.

Lois Sather at Country Quilting for quilting *Butterfly Garden*.

Barb Simons at Stone Ridge Quilting for quilting the *Laundry-Basket Quilt, Tiptoe Through the Flowers, Picnic Quilt* and others.

Margy Manderfeld for letting me use her "Perfect Fit" binding technique.

about the author

Darlene Zimmerman is the author of 7 books for Krause Publications. She has been designing fabrics since 1997 and since 2007 has produced two to six lines each year for Robert Kaufman. Darlene publishes approximately four patterns each year that are distributed through various outlets, including Checker, Nancy's Notions and numerous catalogues. She attends Quilt Market on behalf of Robert Kaufman and EZ Quilting/Simplicity (with whom she has a line of branded tools), and she teaches at quilt guilds and shops around the country. You can visit Darlene at her website, www.feedsacklady.com.

www.fwmedia.com

15   14   13   12   11   5   4   3   2   1

DISTRIBUTED IN CANADA BY FRASER DIRECT
100 Armstrong Avenue
Georgetown, ON, Canada L7G 5S4
Tel: (905) 877-4411

DISTRIBUTED IN THE U.K. AND EUROPE BY F&W MEDIA INTERNATIONAL
Brunel House, Newton Abbot, Devon, TQ12 4PU, England
Tel: (+44) 1626 323200, Fax: (+44) 1626 323319
Email: enquiries@fwmedia.com

DISTRIBUTED IN AUSTRALIA BY CAPRICORN LINK
P.O. Box 704, S. Windsor NSW, 2756 Australia
Tel: (02) 4577-3555

SRN: W0937
ISBN-10: 1-4402-1775-0
ISBN-13: 978-1-4402-1775-3

Edited by Julie Hollyday & Bethany Anderson
Designed by Megan Richards
Cover designed by Julie Barnett
Production coordinated by Greg Nock
Photography by Al Parrish, Richard Deliantoni and Christine Polomsky

Metric Conversion Chart

To convert	to	multiply by
Inches	Centimeters	2.54
Centimeters	Inches	0.4
Feet	Centimeters	30.5
Centimeters	Feet	0.03
Yards	Meters	0.9
Meters	Yards	1.1

Needle? Thread? Fabric?

You're ready to go at **Store.MarthaPullen.com!** Find inspiration and instruction for all stitchers, whether you sew by machine or hand!

A COMMUNITY OF CRAFTERS

Join us on Facebook:
www.facebook.com/fwcraft

Follow us on Twitter: **@fwcraft**

Share with us on Flickr:
www.flickr.com/northlightcrafts

Check out these other great quilting titles by Krause Publications!

Sensational Small Quilts
There's a little something for every quilter in Sensational Small Quilts! Break out of the box by 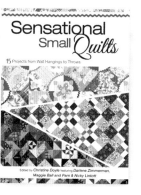 tackling modern quilts, attack your stash with beautiful scrap creations, and embrace your heritage with traditional blocks. Features 15 quilt projects in an array of styles and colors, in sizes ranging from wallhangings to throws.

 **String Quilt Revival**
String quilts have been around for centuries, but in *String Quilt Revival*, this time-tested artform is given a new life! Learn how to sew a variety of string quilt blocks by following clear step-by-step instructions, and discover a new type of foundation: no-show mesh stabilizer, which minimizes distortion of the blocks and doesn't need to be removed. It's a no-fuss approach to quilting that's sure to become a favorite. Featuring 13 unique string quilting projects that produce beautiful results without the worry of precision piecing.